From reports of sexual marauders in our schools to the latest statistics showing the increased alcohol use by eighth graders, the evidence abounds: our children and our culture are at risk. The answers to these problems, however, do not lie in more government programs. The answers lie in strengthening our families, our neighborhoods, our schools, and our churches.

Mike McManus understands this, and in this insightful and helpful book, *50 Practical Ways to Take Our Kids Back from the World,* he gives parents, teachers, ministers, and anyone else who cares about kids practical recommendations for things that they can do to help our children fight the temptations of the world.

It is a useful, practical, and moral book.

> William J. Bennett
> Co-Director, *Empower America*
> Former Secretary of Education, "drug czar," and Chairman of the National Endowment for the Humanities

We have lost the spiritual, moral anchor that secured our nation from its earliest, critical days. We are at sea without compass, direction, or destination.

With the heart of a father, the overview of a commentator, and the skill of a seasoned writer, Michael McManus guides his reader through proven, workable, winnable ways to combat this anarchy. With an abundance of statistics he dramatizes the need. His response to the facts is drawn from experiences that worked for his family, experiences common to most families in past generations.

> Dr. Richard Halverson
> Chaplain, U.S. Senate

50

f i f t y

Practical Ways to Take Our Kids Back from the World

Michael J. McManus

Tyndale House Publishers, Inc.
WHEATON, ILLINOIS

Other books by Michael J. McManus

Introduction to *The Final Report of the Attorney General's Commission on Pornography.* Nashville, Tennessee: Rutledge Hill Press, 1986.
Marriage Savers: Helping Your Friends and Family Stay Married. Grand Rapids, Michigan: Zondervan Publishing House, 1993.

Library of Congress Cataloging-in-Publication Data

McManus, Michael J.
   50 practical ways to take our kids back from the world / Michael J. McManus.
     p.   cm.
   Includes index.
   ISBN 0-8423-1242-0 (soft cover) :
   1. Child rearing—Religious aspects—Christianity. 2. Parenting—Religious aspects—Christianity. I. Title. II. Title: Fifty practical ways to take our kids back from the world.
HQ769.3.M42   1993
649'.1—dc20   93-4596

Printed in the United States of America

99 98 97 96 95 94 93
9   8   7   6   5   4   3   2   1

To the REVEREND EVERETT L. (*Terry*) FULLAM,
who had a greater impact on my life than any other man.
As rector of St. Paul's Episcopal Church, Darien, Connecticut,
he opened the pages of Scripture to me and my family,
making relevant the words of prophets and apostles
about the character of God the Father, Son, and Holy Spirit.
His sermons inspired me to begin writing both of my
syndicated columns, especially "Ethics & Religion," as a
way I might use my talents to serve the Lord.

Contents

CHAPTER EIGHT
Build Future Leaders 245

CHAPTER NINE
Encourage Selfless Service 265

F o r e w o r d

"The impact that family disintegration has on children's lives is a national crisis. The time for silence is over." Thus Mortimer B. Zuckerman, editor-in-chief of *U.S. News and World Report,* in his editorial of April 12, 1993, establishes a critical agenda for America. But, though it is critical, it is not yet hopeless. In this book, author Michael J. McManus presents fifty ways to respond to this critical agenda. As a writer, he articulates with clarity. As a nationally syndicated columnist, he has the big picture. As a father, he addresses his subject in down-to-earth, practical ways. Whatever other responses will be suggested for this national agenda, these from McManus command serious attention and action.

Overwhelmingly, statistics about divorce, single parenthood, teenage problems, and child abuse indicate an alarming decline in the American social order. All the symptoms of paganism are manifest in our culture: hedonism, love of comfort, selfishness, greed, child sacrifice, violence, moral and ethical anarchy. We have lost our way as a people, and we are paying a terrible price—the disintegration of our way of life. Freedom without responsibility, choice without consequence, liberty without law—or perhaps, more precisely, the legalization of anarchy—have become our way of life.

We have lost the spiritual, moral anchor that secured our nation from its earliest, critical days. We are at sea without compass, direction, or destination.

With the heart of a father, the overview of a commentator, and the skill of a seasoned writer, Michael McManus guides his reader through proven, workable, winnable ways to combat this anarchy. With an abundance of statistics he dramatizes the need. His response to the facts is drawn from experiences that worked for his family, experiences common to most families in past generations.

This suggests the wisdom of a seminary professor who often discussed the "rowboat philosophy" of life. In a rowboat, one goes forward by facing backward. He supported this view by reminding us that, though we face forward when driving an automobile, a rear-view mirror is absolutely essential in modern traffic. It's important to know what's behind us as well as what's before us. We ignore the past to our peril.

Out of his own experiences, the author reminds us of things as they once were. He recalls a guided, motivated childhood in which he was loved. This gave purpose to life and eventually led him to success in his profession. Such direction and encouragement are what many children are missing today.

It is indisputable that a culture cannot long endure the disintegration of marriage, family, and home. The family is central to the preservation and perpetuation of humanity, basic to social order, and the primary environment for instruction and growth. God's instruction to the people of Israel included the responsibility to give religious instruction to their families (see Deuteronomy 6:4-9). In the family, value systems are established; authority, discipline, love, and respect are learned; life's direction is set. It is not incidental that family values became an issue in the 1992 presidential election and that more and more publications are devoting space to this issue.

In the editorial with which this foreword began, editor Zuckerman writes, "The developing child needs love, stability, constancy, harmony, and permanence in family life. These needs have been caustically sacrificed in the adult's quest for freedom, independence, and choice. The mantra should be this . . . 'Marriage matters.'" McManus believes that marriage *does* matter, and he demonstrates this in sharing his own experience as husband and father.

Zuckerman continues, "Children in single-parent families are six times as likely as children in two-parent families to be poor, two to three times as likely to have emotional and behavioral problems, more likely to drop out of school, to be expelled or suspended from school, more likely to get pregnant as teenagers, and more likely to use drugs and be in trouble with the law." For economic reasons, if for no other, taxpayers ought to consider the enormous cost such circumstances impose upon us.

From the pen of Michael J. McManus comes

50 Practical Ways to Take Our Kids Back from the World, addressing such statistics philosophically and realistically. With thoughtful hindsight and an accurate perception of the present situation, the author provides his reader with a workable strategy to meet the crisis all of us face. With a profound sense of the need for a spiritual foundation, the essential basis of his "50 ways," the author sets a course that is easily followed and eminently qualified to meet the desperate crisis confronting America.

Richard C. Halverson

Acknowledgments

A few years after I began writing syndicated newspaper columns in 1977, I dreamed of publishing a collection of them as a book. One publisher after another turned me down, saying, "Books of newspaper columns don't sell very well." Therefore, I am particularly grateful to LaVonne Neff, one of Tyndale's acquisitions directors, who sought me out after hearing of my work from Roy Beck, a journalist and friend. She looked at a group of columns I had written about how to guide young people in these tumultuous times, and envisioned this book. She was also open to my writing fresh introductions to each chapter and has been a superb editor. Carole Johnson, one of the working editors on the manuscript, has also been patient and constructive. Both have been a joy to work with.

I am grateful to my wife, Harriet, who had hundreds of ideas on how to brighten the language or the clarity of the fifty answers offered in this book. More important, she has been a wonderful mother to our three sons, Adam, John, and Timothy—creating many of the answers described in this book.

I also want to thank Dr. Richard Halverson, who took time out from his duties as Chaplain of the U.S. Senate to write his gracious foreword. The reader will be interested to know that, as the former pastor of Fourth Presbyterian Church, he developed the outstanding youth program described in Answer 25. Dr. Halverson is a giant reminder that we stand on the shoulders of pioneers who have gone before us.

Finally, I want to thank the editors of two hundred newspapers who have published either my economic/political column, "Solutions," or my "Ethics & Religion" column over the years. Had they not been willing to publish these columns as they were written, you would not be holding this book in your hand.

Why Take Our Kids Back from the World?

Never has it been harder to be an American teenager than in the 1990s. Never has it been harder to be the parent of a teen. I have only to compare today's situation with life in the 1950s, when I was a teenager.

Drinking. In the fifties our big illicit activity was to have a beer, but I can remember only a few classmates who actually got drunk. Today, by contrast, the surgeon general reports that 10.6 million of the nation's 20.6 million seventh- through twelfth-graders drink. Eight million do so weekly; one million, daily. Half a million teens consume fifteen drinks per week.

During the last month, more than 3 million teenagers have indulged in "binge drinking"—having five or more drinks in a brief time. During the last two weeks, 30 percent of high school seniors, one-third of all female college students, and *half* of all male college students have binged.

The price of teen drunkenness is high: 4.5 million of the nation's 18 million alcoholics are young people. In fact, alcohol is the leading cause of death for those aged sixteen to twenty-four, mainly from drunk driving.

Pornography. Pornography was largely unavailable to young people in the fifties. I recall when *Playboy* began to appear on magazine racks; however, there were no X-rated movies or adult bookstores, and no hard-core videos, all-sex cable channels, or top-less bars.

Today 46 percent of junior-high students and 84 percent of high schoolers have seen X-rated movies. Many are not simply graphic portrayals of normal sexual behavior. One sex shop visited by the Pornography Commission had forty-six films and videos featuring bestiality. In addition, they had a whole assortment of depictions of other kinds of kinky sex: urination or defecation on a sexual partner, for example, or various forms of mutilation (fishhooks through genitals, fists in rectums, mousetraps on breasts). Our children are being introduced to perversions, in many cases, even before they are introduced to normal sex.

Divorce. When I was growing up, all my friends lived with both parents, as did I. In the evenings my dad and I would talk for hours about his business, politics, religion, and the news of the day. To keep up with him, I started reading his *Time* magazines, and this eventually inspired me to become a *Time* correspondent (a dream I achieved at age 22). Ours was by no means a perfect home. Dad was an alcoholic, and occasionally when he got drunk, he beat my mom. But our home was intact, and I knew I was loved.

My experience was not unique for the fifties. Only a few among my parents' acquaintances had been divorced, and I never even heard of single-parent families until I worked as a reporter. In 1960 only 9 percent of children under age eighteen were living with only their mothers. But in three decades that figure has nearly tripled, skyrocketing from 5.1 million youngsters in 1960 to 14.6 million in 1991, with another 2 million children living with only their fathers.

"This nation has the highest divorce rate in the world," said the National Commission on Children in 1991. Today, 60 percent of kids see their father walk away from the family. (Even in intact families, fathers tend not to get involved with the kids: the average child spends only five minutes a day talking to Dad.) In 1960 there were only 390,000 divorces. By 1980 there were nearly 1.2 million, a tripling in less than a generation. Divorces plateaued at that level through 1992, when there were 1,192,000. Every year a million kids see their parents divorce.

The problem for most kids does not end with seeing parents divorce. After the divorce Mother and Dad are likely to start dating and then living with one or more partners (nearly half of cohabiting couples have children). If there is a new marriage, there will likely be problems with the stepparent. That is often a factor in the 60 percent divorce rate of second marriages.

Violence. When I went to junior and senior high school, there were occasional fights (I was in only one). But I never heard of teachers being threatened or physically attacked, or of students bringing weapons to school. Schools were safe, happy places.

The National Educational Goals Report of 1992 paints quite a different picture. Violence is rampant in our nation's high schools. It is even worse in junior high schools. In 1991, 16 percent of twelfth-graders were threatened with a weapon; among eighth-graders, 17 percent of whites, 22 percent of Hispanics, and 27 percent of blacks were similarly threatened. Fifteen percent of twelfth-graders and 25 percent of eighth-graders were physically assaulted; 7 percent of twelfth-graders and 9 percent of eighth-graders were injured with a weapon. Among teachers, 19 percent were verbally abused, 8 percent were threatened with injury, and 2 percent were physically attacked.

No wonder former president Bush and all fifty governors agreed to this national goal: "By the year 2000, every school in America will be free of drugs and violence and will offer a disciplined environment conducive to learning." According to the National Educational Goals Report, schools have a long way to go.

Teen Pregnancy. Only a few girls dropped out of my high school because of pregnancy. I never heard of any peer getting an abortion while I was in high school. However, since abortion was illegal at that time, and since I was male, my tender ears may have been protected from what was going on. In fact, there were only 59,000 births to unmarried teenagers in 1950. But by 1991, 518,000 teens gave birth; 339,000 of these were unmarried. That's nearly a sixfold increase from my era. In addition, more than 400,000 teens every year have abortions.

Illegitimacy. Not only are teens giving birth to illegitimate children; many of today's schoolkids themselves are children of never-married mothers. In 1960 there were only 243,000 children living with a never-married parent. By 1991 that figure soared twentyfold to 5.6 million youngsters. And the numbers continue to soar. More than a million children a year are born out of wedlock (slightly more than the number of children each year whose homes are broken by divorce). In just one decade, the 1980s, illegitimacy increased 75 percent. Last year 28 percent of U.S. babies were born to unmarried women.

What is the effect upon society when divorce rates and illegitimacy rates are high? Fatherless families are six times as likely to be poor, to have delinquent children, and to have children with profound learning problems. As Karl Zinsmeister wrote in *The American Enterprise:*

> There is a mountain of scientific evidence showing that when families disintegrate,

children often end up with intellectual, physical, and emotional scars that persist for life. . . . We talk about the drug crisis, the education crisis, and the problems of teen pregnancy and juvenile crime. But all of these ills trace back predominantly to one source— broken families.

Drugs. I first heard of marijuana when I was a senior at Duke University in 1963. Today a fifth of high school seniors have used marijuana. Cocaine was unheard of in the fifties and sixties. By 1980 it had been tried by 16 percent of teens. According to the National Parents Resource Institute for Drug Education (PRIDE), "more than half of the cocaine-using high school seniors began drinking beer and smoking cigarettes at age thirteen or under, and a third began at eleven or under." There may be some good news, however: since 1981 both marijuana and cocaine use among teens have decreased by more than 50 percent.

Lack of Limits. Before the late sixties, colleges assumed some responsibility for the final years of adolescence by acting *in loco parentis* (in place of a parent) to set some limits on college youth. Parents were grateful, and students did not generally feel oppressed by the rules. When I went to college from 1958 to 1963, for example, female students had to be in their dorms by midnight on Fridays and by 1:00 a.m. on Saturdays. My fraternity had a party every week. My fraternity brothers were not all virgins, of course. Yet I don't know of a single fraternity brother who had sex with a girl in his room. I was president of that fraternity, and I knew what was going on.

Today there are no rules. My first son, who also went to Duke, often came back to his room to find his roommate in bed with a girl. He had to choose between being a voyeur or sleeping in a lounge. Date rape is becoming a major campus crisis. Campus health services are trying to figure out how to protect students from AIDS.

Parents worry. Students are at risk. But so far, few are suggesting bringing back the old concept of *in loco parentis*. Boston University, however, is trying a 21st-century version with their Residence Hall Guest Policy, which "ensures that all students living in University housing are provided an environment that is conducive to study and the pursuit of academic and personal growth." It has not brought back chastity, but it has cut promiscuity sharply.

According to the policy, visitors are expected to leave the residences 1:00 A.M. Monday through Friday and 2:30 A.M. Saturday and Sunday. Students may request an overnight guest privilege after receiving consent of their roommates. But this may happen only five times per semester. Though student activists oppose the guest policy, polls show that most students favor it, and this year's applications are higher than ever—20,000 for 3,800 freshman slots.

"The Forces of Social Decomposition"

The difficulty of a parent's task in today's culture was made starkly clear in the opening paragraphs of a 1993 report called "The Index of Leading Cultural Indicators" by Dr. William J. Bennett, who served in the Reagan and Bush administrations first as chairman of the National Endowment for the Humanities, then as secretary of education, and finally as "drug czar." Several paragraphs are worth quoting here:

> Over the last three decades we have experienced substantial social regression. Today the forces of social decomposition are challenging—and in some instances, overtaking—the forces of social composition. And when decomposition takes hold, it exacts an enormous human cost.
>
> Since 1960, population has increased 41 percent; the Gross Domestic Product has nearly tripled; and total social spending by all levels of government (measured in constant 1990 dollars) has risen from $143.73 billion to $787 billion—more than a fivefold increase. Inflation-adjusted spending on welfare has increased 630 percent, and inflation-adjusted spending on education has increased 225 percent. . . .
>
> But during the same thirty-year period there has been a 560 percent increase in violent crime, more than a 400 percent increase in illegitimate births, a tripling of divorces, a

tripling of the percentage of children living in single-parent homes, more than a 200 percent increase in the teenage suicide rate, and a drop of almost 80 points in the S.A.T. scores. Modern-day pathologies, at least great parts of them, have gotten worse. They seem impervious to government spending on their alleviation, even very large amounts of spending. . . .

In the summer of 1990 a special commission of prominent political medical, education and business leaders issued a report, titled *Code Blue*, on the health of America's teenagers. They wrote that "never before has one generation of American teenagers been less healthy, less cared for, or less prepared for life than their parents were at the same age." According to the Commission, the explanation for teenagers' deteriorating condition lies *with their behavior.*

Over the years teachers have been asked to identify the top problems in America's public schools. In 1940 teachers identified talking out of turn, chewing gum, making noise, running in halls, cutting in line, dress code infractions, and littering. When asked the same question in 1990, teachers identified drug abuse, pregnancy, suicide, rape, robbery, and assault. . . .

According to pollster Daniel Yankelovich, our society now places less value than before on what we owe others as a matter of moral obligation; less value on sacrifice as moral good; less value on social conformity, respectability, and observing the rules; and less value on correctness and restraint in matters of physical pleasure and sexuality. Higher value is now placed on things like self-expression, individualism, self-realization, and personal choice.

. . . Aleksandr Solzhenitsyn, in a speech earlier this year, said, 'the West . . . has been undergoing an erosion and obscuring of high moral and ethical ideals. The spiritual axis of life has grown dim.'"

A Long, Dark Corridor to Adulthood

Today's teenagers face a dangerous—but tempting—world. In *Children at Risk* Dr. James Dobson suggests it might be "helpful to think of today's teenager as being compelled to walk alone down a long, dark corridor leading toward adulthood."

On either side of this gloomy hall are many large doors, each bearing identifying words at eye level. They are called *Alcohol, Marijuana, Hard Drugs, Pornography, Gambling, Homosexual Experience, Premarital Sex,* on and on. Every form of addictive behavior is represented by at least one door which the teenager must pass on his journey to maturity. As he approaches each portal, he can hear boisterous laughter and gaiety from within.

His friends—or people he *wants* as friends—
are already inside, and they are obviously
having a blast. Every now and then he hears
someone call his name and beckon him to
the party. Who knows what unimaginable
thrills and sensations and sense of belonging
can be waiting behind one of the doors?
And why shouldn't he experience what everyone else is doing? Who—tell me—who has
the right to keep him locked out there in
the dark by himself? His parents? That's a
laugh.

They had their day, now it's his turn. Brilliant
light shines from under each door, and the
shadows of dancing bodies cast an eerie reflec-
tion on his adolescent face. Pounding music
throbs in his ears. That does it! Forget the consequences! He reaches for the doorknob.*

Evil Surrounds Our Kids

I wrote a book this year called *Marriage Savers*. In it
I suggested ways to
  • avoid a bad marriage
  • strengthen existing marriages
  • save 80 to 90 percent of those headed
    toward divorce
One of my first chapters is devoted to teenagers.
Why? "When 1.1 million teens get pregnant a
year, they are *not* learning discipline needed for

*Dr. James Dobson and Gary Bauer, *Children at Risk: The
Battle for the Hearts and Minds of Our Kids* (Irving, Texas: Word,
1990), 6-7.

lifelong marriage. Rather, promiscuity is preparing them for divorce or welfare!" I wrote.

> Our modern world is chewing up teenagers and spitting them out. Evil surrounds them and is far more pervasive than when teenagers of my generation were growing up. . . . The world seems determined to infect the bodies, the minds, and the souls of our children, making it almost impossible for them to learn self-discipline and selflessness needed for lasting marriage.*

What Kinds of Questions Does This Book Answer?

I try to take on the toughest questions facing parents and kids and point to paths of hope.

After more than three decades as a journalist, I am convinced Paul was absolutely correct when he wrote to the Romans: "We know that in all things God works for the good of those who love him, who have been called according to his purpose" (8:28).

Paul does not mean that everything that happens is good. Rather, he means that even in what appears to be a horrible situation, people of faith can find God working for good in their lives. This book suggests answers for tough questions like these:

*Michael J. McManus, *Marriage Savers: Helping Your Family and Friends Stay Married* (Grand Rapids, Michigan: Zondervan, 1993), 59, 82.

- How can parents whose relationship is stale or shaky rebuild their marriage—indeed, fall back in love with one another at a deeper level—for their sake as well as for their kids?
- How can a parent protect children from pedophiles (child molesters)?
- How can a father and son, or a mother and daughter, build an unshakable bridge of communication as the youngster enters adolescence?
- How can ethics be taught to youth in different settings: a summer camp, a public school, a university?
- What does a strong youth program in a church look like? And if one's own church program for kids is weak, how can Christian values be taught to the children?
- How can a persuasive case be made to teenagers to remain sexually chaste or to become "second-time virgins"?
- How can America's religious history be taught in public schools that have all but excluded it from textbooks?
- What simple but almost never-applied policy can reduce teen mortality, teen promiscuity, and auto insurance rates?
- How can illegitimate children find a loving Christian home?
- How can a college-age son or daughter be persuaded to consider something as selfless as missionary service?

Fifty Practical Ways to Take
Our Kids Back from the World

Because of the danger and evil of the world we live in, we parents need a strategy to recapture our God-given spiritual authority to protect and "train up" our children. I am no child psychologist or expert— only a parent and columnist who has looked for answers. Perhaps a hundred of my columns over the past sixteen years have focused on youth, and on how we as parents, teachers, or church leaders might be able to help them through tempestuous times.

This book contains updated versions of some of the best of my nationally syndicated columns. Some ideas are drawn from the "Solutions" column I wrote for editorial pages for fourteen years. In writing those columns, I pledged to my editors that I would not describe a problem unless I also suggested an answer. The same philosophy undergirds my second nationally syndicated column, "Ethics and Religion," which I still write weekly. The "Fifty Practical Ways" I am suggesting here are largely drawn from these two columns, although all of them have been thoroughly checked and revised, where necessary, to reflect today's realities.

Many of the columns make practical suggestions on what parents can do to equip their kids for life and protect them from an unforgiving world. I have arranged the columns in nine chapters by topic, and I have written fresh introductions to each cluster of columns. In these chapter introductions you will find current data and additional thoughts about how to take our kids back from the world.

In this chapter I've included only three initial pieces to suggest several broad-based practical ways to take our kids back from the world. The "50 Practical Ways" will follow in chapters 2 through 9.

The first column in this chapter reports my shock to discover that my boys' adolescence—what should be a protected time of nurture and slow growth into maturity—was being threatened by societal pressures I never had to face at their age.

The second column is based on the second "Ethics and Religion" column I ever wrote. In it I gave strong evidence from a Gallup poll that teens have a strong—but often unfilled—spiritual hunger, and that many of them find organized religion to be spiritually lifeless.

Eleven years after that 1981 report, Gallup showed that teens no longer distrust organized religion. A Gallup report in 1992 said, "Teens generally give high marks to the youth groups, religious instruction and youth ministers." One myth is that teenagers go to youth groups only to meet members of the opposite sex. "Some do," Gallup reports, "but more say they go because it helps them to deal with their problems and worries or to gain better understanding of their religion." On the other hand, Gallup also reports that only 39 percent of church-attending teens believe abstinence is the answer to AIDS, and 45 percent of recent church attenders strongly support distribution of condoms in high school. How effective is

your church youth group? How would it answer
Gallup's questions?

What are the most important steps we parents
can take to inoculate our children—particularly
very young ones—from the world's siren song?
The third column in this chapter outlines practical
suggestions by Gary Bauer, president of the Family
Research Council in Washington, D.C.

We parents can and must take our children back
from the world. There are probably as many ways
to do this as there are parents. I hope the fifty in
this book will give a lot of parents a running start.

Our Kids Are Growing Up Too Fast

I knew times had changed when my three teenage
boys began getting calls from girls, which had
never happened to my brother or me when we
were young. One particular weekend I discovered
just how drastic the change was.

My thirteen-year-old received a call at 11:10 Sunday night. My outraged wife picked up the phone
to see who would call at such an hour, only to
accidentally overhear a snippet of what the young
girl on the other end had to say: "You know M——?
How would you like to f—— her?"

I suddenly felt that my boys' adolescence—a
protected time of nurture and slow growth into
maturity—was being robbed from them by societal
pressures that I never had to face at their age.
When I mentioned to my wife that I might write
about this, she urged me to read *All Grown Up & No
Place To Go* by David Elkind, a professor of child

study at Tufts University (Redding, Mass.: Addison-Wesley, 1984).

Buy it for yourself or your spouse. Here are some excerpts:

> There is no place for teenagers in American society today—not in our homes, not in our schools, and not in society at large. This was not always the case. Barely a decade ago . . . teenagers received the time needed to adapt to the remarkable transformation their bodies, minds and emotions were undergoing. . . .
>
> Teenagers have lost their once privileged position. Instead, they have had a premature adulthood thrust upon them. Teenagers now are expected to confront life and its challenges with the maturity once expected only of the middle-aged. . . . Some parents are so involved in reordering their lives, managing a career, marriage, parenting, and leisure that they have no time to give their teenagers. . . .
>
> The media and merchandisers, too, no longer abide by the unwritten rule that teenagers are a privileged group who require special protection and nurturing. They now see teenagers as fair game for all the arts of persuasion and sexual innuendo once directed only at adult audiences and consumers.
>
> High schools, which were once the setting for a unique teenage culture and language, have become miniatures of the adult community. Theft, violence, sex, and substance abuse

are now as common in the high schools as they are on the streets.

And what are the consequences of this imposition of premature adulthood?

Elkind sees three kinds of new stress on teens that we adults did not face a generation ago:

- More freedom than before—in available sex, liquor, drugs, etc.
- More loss than before—divorces have tripled since 1960, causing sudden, permanent loss for half of today's kids; optimism for the future has been replaced by worry about job insecurity, pollution, depletion of resources, nuclear war, etc.
- More failure—because of excessive pressure to "be successful," to excel academically, in sports, music, or extracurricular activities in order to "get into good schools"; kids themselves want desperately to be popular and will do things they know are wrong.

Some statistics reveal the grim result:

- Alcohol and drug abuse is the leading cause of teenage death, accounting for ten thousand deaths a year. A Massachusetts governor's survey of five thousand kids in seventy-three public and private high schools revealed that two of three juniors have used illicit drugs, and 40 percent in the last month. In Greenwich, Connecticut, 57 percent of seniors are drinking weekly and 36 percent "get drunk once a week."

- Sexual activity has grown fivefold. Twenty years ago, only 10 percent of girls were "sexually active" (to use the current fashionable term for fornicating), but now 50 percent are "active today," says Elkind. So 1.1 million become pregnant, a third of whom have and keep their babies while the rest are aborted.
- Suicide rates have tripled in a generation.

Fortunately, there are some answers to this continuing madness. They can be summed up in a single sentence: Every adult must do what he or she can to stretch out those adolescent years, offering both protection and wholesome nurturing.

"The first and most basic thing we can do as parents to help young people," says Elkind, "is to say no. . . . It is easier to give in. But we pay an inordinate price for giving in. Teenagers will fight limits and rules. . . . But giving in to pressure is a losing game. Deal with principle, not with pressure."

No liquor or beer at teens' parties, nor attendance by teens at parties where it is to be served. No *Playboy* subscriptions. No cable TV with porno channels in the home. No attendance by kids at R-rated movies, since the films are likely to contain either open sexual intercourse or excessive violence. Even PG-13 movies are off limits in my house, for such a rating was given to *Red Dawn*, which averaged 134 different violent acts per hour.

We also do everything we can to protect our boys from adolescent sexual experience, while giving them opportunities to be with girls in chaperoned situations. So there are plenty of dancing lessons, weekly church fellowships, retreats, and even a ski weekend with talks on religious and moral themes at night.

Moreover, we try to present a solid rational case for chastity, on both biblical and practical grounds. "Flee from sexual immorality. All other sins a man commits are outside his body, but he who sins sexually sins against his own body" (1 Cor. 6:18), I read to my thirteen-year-old boy after the phone incident.

"Twenty million young people have herpes, says *Time* magazine," I added. "Further, a teenager is not old enough for the emotional involvement, let alone parenting."

Will our stand make a difference? I don't know, but we are doing everything we can to prevent the tides of early adulthood from sweeping our teens away.

Churches Must Meet Teens' Needs

After years of polling the pulse of America, George Gallup, Jr., has developed a thesis on what can be done to deal with one of the deepest sources of pain in families—the turning of young people to drugs, alcohol, sexual promiscuity, and bizarre religious cults.

The churches of America must shift their all-too-frequent focus on organizational and financial matters toward cultivating much deeper spiritual roots, with new methods of outreach to the most neglected segment of the church body, teen-agers.

"Clearly the deep spiritual hunger of young people is not being met by the established church," says Gallup in a thoughtful book coau-thored with Rev. David Polling, *The Search for America's Faith*. What's the evidence of that hunger in an age when a million teenagers become pregnant annually, and there are half as many divorces as marriages, and one abortion for every two live births?

"Nearly nine out of ten teenagers pray, an extraordinarily high proportion believe in God (or a universal spirit), and only one out of a hundred says that he or she does not have some kind of reli-gious preference or affiliation," say the authors.

However, they add that "this group indicates dis-tance from organized religion, frustration over the church's role in society, and a generally negative attitude toward churchgoers."

In his report, *Religion in America 1979–80*, Gallup summarizes the paradox this way: "Young people appear to be spiritually restless; they want a strong religious faith, but at the same time find organized religion to be spiritually lifeless. As a result they are intrigued by the para-normal and by unconventional religions and cults."

If the nation's 25 million teenagers are to be reached with the kind of help that will enable them to navigate through a "permissive society that has no enforced standards regarding alcohol usage, sexual experimentation and social responsibility," Gallup says that "parents must first be reached."

"Our survey evidence suggests strongly that many families in this country desperately need help—spiritual help. Too many Americans belong to a category of 'not-quite-Christians' who believe, but without strong convictions; who want the rewards of the faith without the obligation. . . . Many parents and children alike are 'spiritual illiterates.' A significant proportion (in the case of Christians) can articulate in the most vague fashion the significance of the resurrection of Jesus Christ for mankind.

"And while most homes have at least one Bible, many Americans have not learned how to bring the Bible into their lives. Few can name the four Gospels or more than the first few of the Ten Commandments."

So what?

Gallup has found a direct correlation between the strength of a person's religious life, and his overall health. In fact, years of using his sophisticated polling techniques has enabled Gallup to amass incontrovertible evidence that, as he puts it, "Religion does, indeed, make a difference."

Religious people are about 50 percent more likely to agree with these two important statements than people who don't go to church:

1. "Facing my daily tasks is a course of pleasure and satisfaction."
2. "I have discovered clear-cut goals and a satisfying life purpose."

The problem is that the number of people who say that religion is "very important" in their lives was as high as 75 percent in 1952, but plunged to only 53 percent in 1980. By 1991, however, it rose to 58 percent, the highest figure since 1965. The biggest drops are among young people, only a quarter of whom attend church on a Sunday (compared to 40 percent of adults). Three-fourths of the young "believe a person can be a good Christian even if he or she does not go to church."

But the situation is not hopeless, if one listens to the complaints of the young about the church. Many young people have high standards that the church doesn't meet!

"Some 40 percent believed the church was failing to do its proper job in society through its neglect of the poor and underprivileged, its spiritual apathy, its excessive materialism, its hypocritical stance, its out-of-date approach to youth, and its avoidance of moral problems," said the authors.

An in-depth survey in Dayton revealed these blunt comments: "The church . . . tries to save the world while people in the church go to hell," said a young Presbyterian. "They're too worried about building finer churches and not worried enough about doing what the church was set up for," complained a United Church of Christ member.

"They spend too much time preaching birth control, abortion, and such and do nothing to help those who need understanding and counseling," fumed another.

There's a righteousness to this outrage, which is

encouraging. The young don't lack faith. But they are "growing up with little familiarity with the Bible, little conviction about sin and the need for repentance—and, in the case of Christians—without sensing the joy of a close personal relationship with Christ," says Gallup.

Finding no answers in the traditional church, 6 million teenagers have turned to yoga, Eastern religions, transcendental meditation, etc. Far more seek answers in drugs, alcohol, and sexual relationships. Four of every ten fourteen-year-old girls will become pregnant during their teenage years. Half will give birth while the rest have abortions.

What can the churches do? "The young indicate that they want to go deep into the great places of God through prayer, Bible study, and personal discipline," say the authors. "Recreation, activities, and entertainment are way down on the urgency scale."

Yet most churches have no special ministries to teenagers. Half of those polled would welcome the opportunity to attend spiritual retreats. Similar numbers "have a very powerful social consciousness," says Gallup. He suggests that churches enable the young to visit the sick and the shut-ins, or care for the young.

What is your church doing to reach America's neglected teenagers?

Our Children Need to Be Taught Traditional Values

What was the best thing about your Christmas—the presents you received or the love with which they were given and the reknitting of your family? Of course, family joy was more important.

This would not surprise Gary Bauer, president of the Family Research Council and former White House director of domestic policy under Reagan. As he wrote in *Our Journey Home:* "Most families endure. After thirty years of 'experimentation' in which old values were tossed overboard," there is a "yearning" among people to return "home."

While the percentage of working mothers with kids under age six shot up from 19 to 59 percent from 1960 to 1990, Bauer cites polls showing that 57 percent of women would "consider giving up work indefinitely" if they "no longer needed the money." That figure is up 18 percent from 1989 to 1990. While two-thirds of baby boomers abandoned the faith of their youth, Bauer notes that one-third returned when they had children of their own.

Many stories of 1992 were about an abandoning of traditional mores: "Magic" Johnson finds he has AIDS caught from a promiscuous sex life; the date-rape cases of William Kennedy Smith and Mike Tyson hit the airwaves; a growing number of schools hand out condoms; Time-Warner defends releasing the rap song "Cop Killer" as freedom of speech; former vice president Quayle touches off a fire storm when he says "Murphy Brown" glamorized having an out-of-wedlock child.

No man was more visible in 1992 articulating old-home values than Gary Bauer. He was on scores of TV shows about the "Murphy Brown" episode alone. Yet *Our Journey Home* is largely not about such public issues—but about what each of us can do in our private life to strengthen our family ties. "I care about government and politics," he told me in an interview. "But the most important things happening in the country happen around dinner tables—where families are, not in the House or Senate."

Any parent can make his or her children's lives more meaningful by considering his ideas:

1. "The most important thing we can teach children is that each human being is a unique creature of God." He says that he and his wife, Carol, have told their three children that "a loving Father who created them cares about them individually," despite any possible physical limitations.

2. "Second, we have tried to teach our children that the most important things can't be bought." When they were disappointed not to go on an "upscale" vacation like some neighbors, Gary told them his own folks "were never able to go on a vacation, nor did we ever own a new car."

More important, each child is taught a personal responsibility to help those less fortunate. Each year their kids go "through their toys and select some to give the needy kids program" run by the U.S. Marines. They also see their parents helping crisis pregnancy centers raise money.

3. "Our children are taught that we unconditionally love them." How? First, by telling them "again and again" and reminding them that "no matter how things come out, they are loved if they bring home *A*'s or *D*s. They are loved if they do well at

sports or if they follow their father's less sterling athletic record. They are loved if they win a school election or if they come in last. I don't believe children instinctively know this.

"In our success-oriented society many kids feel parental love is conditioned on performance. It shouldn't be."

4. "Children must be taught that choices have consequences. The child who opts for television instead of studying the night before an exam will suffer the consequences of a low grade. . . .

5. "Each child should be given reliable standards of right and wrong. Our culture is permeated with the philosophy of relativism." By contrast, he notes Nightline's Ted Koppel told Duke University graduates a few years ago, "What Moses brought down from Mount Sinai were not the Ten Suggestions. They are commandments. Are, not were. The sheer brilliance of the Ten Commandments is that they codify in a handful of words acceptable human behavior, not just for then or now, but for all time."

Finally, the Bauers have found a wonderful way to instill in their children "character to stand against the crowd" and perseverance needed to "overcome almost anything." How? They are read "the literature of family, faith, and freedom" ranging from *The Little Engine that Could* and the *Midnight Ride of Paul Revere,* through the Peter Rabbit series, Hans Christian Anderson, *To Kill a Mockingbird,* and The Chronicles of Narnia.

t   w **2**.

Improve Family Communication

Perhaps the most important way to take our kids back from the world is to improve communication within families. The place to begin is not with the kids at all, but with their parents.

Six out of ten young marriages are dissolving, according to the National Survey of Families and Households. Why? A 1989 Gallup poll reports the cause of divorce in three-fifths of all cases as simply poor communication! In George Gallup's words, "In an era of increasingly fragile marriages, a couple's ability to communicate is the single most important contributor to a stable and satisfying marriage."

But how can communication between husband and wife be improved? Who can teach spouses to communicate? There is no better single answer than a weekend retreat called Marriage Encounter, which I describe in Answer 1.

Do you feel bored or ignored in your marriage, joyless, disillusioned? A million and a half couples have gone on Marriage Encounter, and studies reveal that *90 percent* fall back in love with each other, this time at a far deeper level than before!

Perhaps your marriage is in more desperate straits. Maybe it is already headed for the rocks. Answer 1 suggests a stronger remedy, a weekend retreat called *Retrouvaille* (French for "rediscovery"). Up to half of the couples who attend are already separated or divorced, and yet *80 to 90 percent* of them rebuild their marriages!*

Most parents have fairly good communication with their kids until they reach about age twelve. Then hormones rage, parents scream, and doors slam—including the door to communication.

"How would you like to be thirteen years old again?" asks Dr. James Dobson, a Christian psychologist and author whose daily radio program is heard on two thousand stations nationwide. Most of us would say, "No, thanks." We remember how painful those years could be. How can we help our sons and daughters through those difficult years of early adolescence?

One wonderful answer is called Adolescent Weekend. I describe it in Answer 2. A father and son, or a mother and daughter, go to a special place all alone when the youngster turns twelve. I took all three of my sons away individually to a mountain resort where we played golf for the first time together, swam, fished, and enjoyed long talks. To spark our talks, I turned on one of six tape recordings by Dr. Dobson. We listened together on the way to the resort, while we were there, and again

*To learn more about Marriage Encounter and Retrouvaille, see chapters 9 and 10 of my book *Marriage Savers* (Grand Rapids, Michigan: Zondervan, 1993).

on the way home. Adolescent Weekend turned out to be one of our most memorable experiences. It built a bridge of love and communication that helped me be a better father years later when adolescent pressures were much more intense.

Of course, there is no single inoculation that will immunize your kids from the world. As they become teenagers, temptations are manifold. However, there are some basic rules of communication that parents can learn. I outline them in Answer 3.

One practical way to communicate your values to your kids is to give your high school or college student a subscription to *Campus Life* magazine. Published by the same company that also publishes *Christianity Today*, it is a regular source of hope, information, and tangible help. One of the best features is a regular column by Tim Stafford called "Love, Sex, and the Whole Person," a Christian Ann Landers for teens. You can find more information about *Campus Life* in Answer 4.

In Chapter 1, I stressed that an important parental ally in taking kids back from the world is a good church youth group. But what if your church has an ineffectual group, and what if your communication with your own teen is terrible? Answer 5 suggests involving your teenager in a parachurch ministry called Young Life. I saw it save not only the life of a rebellious girl, but also her relationship with her very angry father.

The sad reality, however, is that "the United States is increasingly a fatherless society," as I wrote in a Father's Day column in 1992. Says one expert, "Fatherlessness is now approaching a rough parity with fatherhood as a defining feature of American childhood." In Answer 6 I suggest the need to reform our no-fault divorce laws, which enable a man to run off with his secretary, divorce his wife, and demand half the value of the house so that, in effect, his wife and kids are subsidizing his illicit affair! In the past, such a man would have had to give up the house and pay alimony.

I suggest a reform that would give couples a two-track marriage system. Couples could choose today's "no fault" system, a *Marriage of Compatibility* that allows either party to quit the marriage without a reason and obtain a 50-50 split of property. Or they might choose to add legal teeth to the vows of their marriage in a *Marriage of Commitment* that would not allow a divorce unless one could prove the partner had broken the marital vows (by adultery, desertion, and the like).*

However, it is a mistake to think that government can bind a man and woman together for life. Only the Lord can do that. He can become the third partner of any marriage, as I explain in Answer 1. And so I call upon pastors to preach on what Scripture says about marriage, divorce, and sex outside marriage. Have you ever heard a sermon on cohabitation (which now precedes most marriages and which increases the odds of divorce by 50 percent)? I have not.

*To learn more, see chapter 11 of my book *Marriage Savers* (Grand Rapids, Michigan: Zondervan, 1993).

National religious denominations have also avoided the issues of marriage and divorce. In a dozen years of covering all major denominations, I have not heard any talk about what might be done to reduce the divorce rate. Curiously, the pressure for reform is coming from *secular* sources. In 1992, conservative and liberal scholars fashioned a "Communitarian Platform" that urged a change in divorce law described in Answer 7: "Two-parent families are better able to discharge their child-raising duties. Though divorces are necessary in some situations, many are avoidable and not in the interest of children."

In 1993, the impact of the Communitarian Platform could be seen in two major developments:

1. Dr. William Bennett, after summarizing his "Index of Leading Cultural Indicators"—giving evidence of "substantial social regression"—came to a similar conclusion as the Communitarian Platform on the need to rescind "no-fault divorce laws for parents with children."

2. *The Atlantic* magazine published an article by Barbara Dafoe Whitehead in April 1993 headlined, "Dan Quayle Was Right." She argues, "The dissolution of two-parent families, though it may benefit the adults involved, is harmful to many children and dramatically undermines our society." For example, "family disruption is best understood not as a single event, but as a string of disruptive events: separation, divorce, life in a single-parent family, life with a parent and live-in lover, the remarriage of one or both parents, life in one

stepparent family combined with visits to another
stepparent family, the breakup of one or both stepparent families." She proposes a "children first"
principle in divorce proceedings, like that suggested by Mary Ann Glendon, now on the staff of
the vice president. "Under this rule, judges in
litigated divorce cases would determine the best
possible package of benefits, income and services
for children. Only then would the judge turn to
other issues such as the division of remaining marital assets. . . . Another idea is to reintroduce some
measure of fault in divorce in awarding alimony."

Oklahoma is working toward a practical way of
putting children first. Its House of Representatives
passed a bill February 22, 1993, that would give
judges the right, in cases involving children, to
order the parents "to submit to counseling, media-
tion or parenting/divorce education." At this writing it had not yet been acted upon by the state
senate.

Is your child anorexic, your husband insuffer-
able? Are your elderly parents a terrible burden?
No matter what the family problem, there is no
better single source of help than Dr. Dobson's
Focus on the Family, which provided personal
assistance to 223,400 people who requested help
in 1991. Focus answers thousands of letters. They
send helpful tapes and books. If the problem is
acute, certified counselors will telephone persons
in need and suggest resources in their own communities. Answer 8 gives a feel for how Focus works.
Since the column was first written, its ministry has

doubled in size. What is important, however, has remained the same: *anyone* seeking advice on *any* issue involving families can receive help *at no cost* simply by writing to Focus on the Family, Colorado Springs, CO 80905.

A n s w e r **1**

"Marriage Encounter" Helps Couples Fall Back in Love

Questions for married readers: Do you feel bored or ignored in your marriage? Has disillusionment replaced romance? Is it a joyless union?

If so, I have a suggestion. Go on a Marriage Encounter weekend.

Dr. James Dobson, the Christian psychologist and author, went "for professional reasons, not expecting to get anything relevant to my wife and me. If there is anything I felt Shirley and I didn't need, it was help in communications. I rarely have been more wrong," he wrote in *Love Must be Tough* (Waco, Tex.: Word, 1983).

In preparation for Worldwide Marriage Encounter's twenty-fifth anniversary, the organization commissioned an extraordinary study to the National Institute of the Family. Couples who attended Marriage Encounter weekends during its first twenty-five-years were asked to rank the quality of their marriage before going. Nearly half said their marriage was "average" to "unhappy."

Yet the study concluded that "the Marriage Encounter Weekend/Program stands as the central positive experience of most couples. . . . Marriage

Encounter is a positive marriage enrichment for nine out of ten couples."

Only 48 of the 325 respondents said they had an excellent marriage before the weekend, but nearly 200 felt that way immediately afterward. Today, even decades later, 100 say their marriage is "excellent"; 145 call it "very good"; and 60 say it is "pretty good." Only 10 of the 325 say their marriage is "the same" and 10 say it's "rather poor."

Furthermore, 1.5 million American couples have made a Marriage Encounter weekend.

To spark deep sharing, three "lead couples" and a priest or pastor and wife share intimate details of their marital struggles with perhaps twenty to forty attending couples. Then each couple goes back to their motel room. The assignment for each is to write a "love letter" to his or her spouse, answering questions like "What do I like best about you?" and "How does it make me feel?" After writing for ten minutes, husband and wife exchange love letters, and talk about them for another ten minutes. These "10 & 10s" happen often. The experience is totally private. Only lead couples share in public.

Two profound principles are taught, or, rather, are caught by attendees:

- "Feelings are neither right nor wrong. They just are. Feelings are the real me. They must be shared," said a leader. For many men this is hard. We've been trained to hold feelings in. Releasing them is cathartic.

- "Love is a decision, not a feeling." If I do
  something special for my wife, I love her
  more. She, then, is more loving to me. So
  the feeling of love—a deep joy—grows. Jesus
  said, "Give, and it will be given to you"
  (Luke 6:38).

I know, firsthand, that the program works. Like
most couples who've gone, my wife and I fell back
in love with one another—and at a far more profound level because of that weekend experience.

My marriage to my wife, Harriet, was under great
stress in 1976. I was commuting from Stamford to
Washington, D.C., getting on the train at 2:00 A.M.
on Monday morning and not coming home until
11:00 P.M. Friday night.

Harriet put up with this graciously for months,
fixing a lovely late dinner on Fridays. Saturdays
and Sundays I was buried in my writing. I was not
a good father or husband.

As the urging of several friends from church who
paid our way and took care of our kids, we went to
a Marriage Encounter weekend. That weekend I
was shocked to learn that Harriet felt "bruised" by
my work in Washington. "You left me for a year
and a half . . . quite voluntarily. . . . I felt deserted,"
she told me. As we talked, she added, "This is no
marriage. I never see you during the week. You
work all the time and don't even take the boys for
a swim. This is not why I married you. You're a
workaholic. You love your work, not me."

I broke down and wept. I had been so absorbed
in the difficulty of my life that I had not realized

its impact on Harriet. I asked her forgiveness. I had not known she was holding this abandoned feeling within her all those months.

That weekend I learned that it is absolutely essential to take time out with one's spouse every day. In the years since then, we have gotten up earlier than usual for unstructured talk, reading of Scripture, and prayer. Christ became a third partner in our marriage.

"There is within each couple a divine energy of love, and it can be brought alive," says Rev. Gabriel Calvo, the Spanish priest who created the program.

If you have not gone on a Marriage Encounter weekend and would like to learn more, call 1-800-795-LOVE. Someone in your area will call you and tell you when the next one will be held. No one is kept away due to a lack of money.

If your marriage is in deep trouble—if it has become unloving, cold and distant, and there is no meaningful communication—a type of Marriage Encounter called *Retrouvaille* (French for "rediscovery") has been created. Couples who've been through hell and survived lead the weekend. Half who go are separated or divorced, yet 80 to 90 percent of the marriages are saved.

Attendees must agree in advance that they want to make their marriage work. If a third party is involved, that relationship must be ended. The lead couples tell attendees how they nearly destroyed their marriage. The person with the biggest sin confesses it openly. Bob told of his unfaithfulness to his wife, Marie. But she acknowledged her part in that she "quit paying attention to him when we had kids. So he went out looking for other relationships."

Such searing honesty does not leave any dry eyes in the room.

More important, their honesty helped Mike and Brenda. Mike had been having affairs whenever he traveled out of town—which was frequently. Then he got reckless and had sex with a neighbor. His wife heard about it, was incredulous, and flew into a furious attack on him in front of their two boys, then aged nine and six. The horrified boys had never seen them argue about anything, let alone adultery. "I regret that my kids saw it," said Brenda. It was the low point of their marriage.

When Brenda and Mike heard Bob and Marie share their story, Mike said, "It was so applicable. You go back to your room and tell each other that you both want the relationship to work. You share your feelings and basically rediscover each other. I found out things I had long forgotten—that we were still friends who still loved each other. We saw couples who had been through so much misery, and how they came out of it and are now shining examples of happy people. That *really* is motivating."

Thus Retrouvaille helps those listening to gain a vision of a healed marriage emerging from disaster; in addition, it gives them the communication tools to work for it and the heart to do so.

The dividends of a healed marriage are immense to one's children. On Mike and Brenda's recent anniversary, their oldest son, now thirteen, who had witnessed the horrifying discovery of his father's adultery, was able to write his parents this deeply moving letter:

> Thank you for being mine and Jacob's parents, and all that you do for me—helping me when needed, driving out of the way for me, taking me places, playing sports and board games, standing up for us, encouraging me to do whatever you think is good, and disciplining me when I have done wrong so I won't do it again. These are some of the things you parents do for us kids. You did it together which really counts.
>
> You stayed together mostly because you did not want to lose us or hurt us, and I respect you for making that decision. You don't know that if we listed all the things you do for me we would be talking or writing the rest of our lives.
>
> Happy Anniversary,
> Jason

Retrouvaille is not yet everywhere. For information, call (713) 455-2027.

2 A n s w e r

Adolescent Weekend Strengthens Parent-Teen Relationships

If you have a child aged ten to fifteen, I'd like to suggest the perfect gift. And if you have no children that age, it is a gift that you can suggest to the

parents of children you love. Reg Jones, a resident
of Darien, Connecticut, and a member of my
church, describes the gift as "the greatest insurance
you can buy for the Christian upbringing of your
children." What is it? We call it an Adolescent
Weekend.

Give your child two complete days of your time
(or that of your spouse) away at a resort where you
can do two things together: have fun and listen to
six extraordinary tapes that are designed to help
your child through the most stressful and threatening time of life—adolescence.

"How would you like to be thirteen years old
again?" asks Dr. James Dobson, a Christian child
psychologist who created the tapes. Almost any
adult will say "No thanks" because they remember their agonizing feelings of those years of
self-doubt, inferiority, and vulnerability to embarrassment, ridicule, or failure with the opposite
sex.

Yet parents don't know how to ease that pain for
their own children. As Reg Jones put it, "I had no
well-conceived idea of how to explain adolescence—growing up—to them. This seemed like a
way to share with a child, but have a professional
explain it. By taking off with a child alone for a
weekend, in our busy lives, that demonstrates how
much you care."

In the first tape, Dr. Dobson explains he will be
talking "about the things teenagers worry about
most." What causes the most hurt and pain is a
feeling of inferiority—"that awful awareness that

nobody likes you, that you are not as good as others."

For example, he notes that 80 percent of teenagers don't like the way they look. Eighty percent! And whatever flaws they may have are often a source of teasing by others. When I took Adam, who was then fourteen, I turned off the tape at that point and told him how terrible I had felt as a teenager because I was so tall—six feet, eight inches—and not a basketball player.

Adam said that by telling stories of my vulnerability, I helped him realize that feelings of inadequacy were universal, so he could talk more openly about his emotions.

Several answers Dr. Dobson suggests are quite practical. "Recognize that you are not alone—inferiority is a common disorder; develop true friends and your natural interests or strengths so that you have something to be proud of." But he also suggests that Christians offer their lives to God in a prayer something like this: "Dear Jesus, I'm asking you to use me in whatever way you wish. Make me the kind of person you want me to be. And from this moment forward, I will not worry about my imperfections."

The next tape deals with pressures to conform—the kind of pressures that lead kids to smoke and to rampant teenage alcoholism. Reg Jones's son, Ross, now sixteen, summed up the situation that twelve-year-olds face in Darien: "When you start in junior high, a lot of conformity starts. Drugs and alcohol start here, and

sexuality. It is a time when your body is changing—an unsure time when you are in a bigger
atmosphere and need a firm base of values to
retreat to."

Dr. Dobson warns his young listeners that it is
almost certain they will be in a car with kids, one of
whom will pop some red pills in his mouth, and
pass them around to others who do the same.
When they are handed to you, what are you going
to say? You know they are harmful to your body,
but you don't want to be laughed at. Now is the
time to decide whether you'll be a "jellyfish." Do
you have enough confidence in yourself to oppose
the group when it is wrong by saying, "No, that's
stupid."

Again, he uses a key Scripture, Paul's letter to the
Romans, which says, "Do not be conformed any
longer to the pattern of this world [or don't let the
world squeeze you into its mold], but be transformed [made into something new] by the renewing of your mind" (12:2).

The third tape deals sensitively with the changes
in the body of both girls and boys, explains sexual
intercourse, and takes the position that premarital
sex is "damaging to the person who engages in it."

The fourth tape is the most profound of all, and is
one people of all ages should hear, for it deals with
misconceptions about love that permeate American
society. As Dr. Dobson puts it, "The high divorce
rate in this country results, in part, from the failure
of newlyweds to understand what love is, what it is
not, and how to make sense out of emotions."

What do kids think about Adolescent Weekend? Adam had a lot to say after our trip:

> You should take John away on his twelfth birthday. I wish I heard the tapes earlier. They are a guide to key issues children deal with daily. In school, the in-crowd's tastes are supposed to be your tastes. A lot of teenagers start smoking or have physical relationships with girls solely for the admiration of their classmates. The tapes bring out the issues where you can discuss them and open up lines of communication between the teenager and the parent. Parents assume that the child knows about infidelity, conformity, and love, so they seldom sit their children down at a preadolescent age, go through the emotions and how to cope with them. On the very sensitive issue of sex, it is better for the parent to discuss what's right and what's wrong rather than leaving that education to schoolmates.

Well, several years later I took Adam's advice and took John on an Adolescent Weekend on his twelfth birthday. The following year I took my youngest son, Tim, to a mountain resort on the weekend of his twelfth birthday.

Most of us parents are reluctant to share our own experience with our kids, primarily, I believe, because we don't know what to say. But Dr. Dobson makes it easy. Adam said about his trip, "Having the tapes along was like having a third

parent along, who opens up communications between a parent and the child. The tapes are like a
corkscrew which pulls the cork out of the bottle,
and unleashes the things which block communication—fear, embarrassment, intimidation."

"He makes you know that everyone has the
same problems," says John. "The Adolescent Weekend also gave us a chance to have some fun
together—going golfing and fishing. The fact you
took me away for two days shows that you cared
about me," he recalled from his trip.

Nevertheless, I had only imperfectly learned Dobson's message that love, to a kid, is spelled T-I-M-E,
until I read his book *Straight Talk to Men and Their
Wives* (Waco, Tex.: Word, 1984). In it, he asks
whether you've heard yourself saying: "Son, we've
been talking about that wagon we were going to
build one of these Saturdays, and I just want you to
know that I haven't forgotten it. But we can't do it
this weekend 'cause I have to make an unexpected
trip to Indianapolis. However, we will get to it one
of these days. I'm not sure if it can be next weekend,
but you keep reminding me."

Dobson continues: "Then the days soon become
weeks, and the weeks flow into months and years
and decades . . . and our kids grow up and leave
home. Then we sit in the silence of our family
rooms, trying to recall the precious experiences that
escaped us there. Ringing in our ears is that haunt-
ing phrase, 'We'll have a good time . . . then.'"

That moved me deeply, for Dobson was describ-
ing my usual experience with my kids. I resolved to

spend a day a week with them doing what they wanted to do.

Unfortunately, half of the nation's children will live part of their lives without any father at home and not feel the love of that father—if present trends continue. Dobson unblinkingly defines the problem as "renegade fathers" who follow not their sacred oath "to love and to cherish, till death do us part," but the siren song of the "me first" philosophy symbolized by such books as *Creative Divorce* and *Looking Out for Number One*.

If you are tempted to abandon your children—or know of others who are—I urge you to get *Straight Talk to Men and Their Wives*.

"To those who have walked away from that responsibility, it is never too late to demonstrate your love. Kids are ready to forgive any father who comes back and says, 'Give me another chance.'" Says who? Dobson? No. That's Representative (now Senator) Dan Coats, R-Indiana, who has become such a Dobson disciple that he has assumed responsibility to introduce other members of Congress to the Christian psychologist's views. He and Representative Frank Wolf, R-Virginia, have gotten many members to watch *Where's Dad?* a powerful Focus on the Family film of Dobson making many of these points.

Their leadership suggests a strategy that other fathers might take to inspire other men to be better fathers. Why not show *Where's Dad?* in your church or corporation? Many communities have even put it on local TV. Make a resolution to be a better father and to help others do so. For information, write Focus on the Family, P.O. Box 35500, Colorado Springs, CO 80935-3550.

A n s w e r **3**

Parents Can Improve Communication with Teens

How can parents communicate their deepest beliefs to their teenagers?

Because today's kids are confronted by so many unhealthy temptations, it is imperative that parents communicate traditional values to them. An annual study of the National Institute on Drug Abuse reveals that 41 percent of high school seniors got drunk in the last two weeks—consuming five or more drinks in a row at one time. Two-thirds say they have used illegal drugs, and suicides are up 300 percent in recent years, and are now a big cause of teenage deaths.

Many parents have tried to communicate their faith to their kids, but without luck in many cases. Why? For most teens "the word 'Christianity' conjures up images of unbelievable miracles, boring ritual, and inhibiting ethics, all shrouded in an aura of dull respectability. The thought that Christianity might be the key which unlocks the meaning of the universe, the pivot point of history, and a wellspring of personal joy, has never occurred to them."

Says who? The Fellowship of Christians in Universities and Schools, better known as FOCUS. This group provides one of the best bridges I've ever seen between the teen, the church, and home. For example, FOCUS sponsored a panel discussion whose title pulled me in: "How Do We Communicate Our Deepest Convictions to the Young?" Rev. Peter Moore, the handsome founder of FOCUS and its former director, summed up the challenge succinctly: "The future of the church will rise or fall on its success with youth.

"FOCUS's goal is to help kids ask basic questions in a way they won't be laughed at. The three big ones are God, sex, and death," he said, noting that FOCUS's usual way of answering those questions is either in small fellowship groups or in such exciting settings as a ski weekend at Williams College or at the FOCUS Study Center in Martha's Vineyard, which can house up to 100 students at a time, within a walk of the beach.

But the parents who came to the panel at Greenwich Academy, an elegant school on an estate once owned by a Rockefeller, wanted to know how they could communicate better with their own kids.

"As teens go from dependence to independence, they must examine all values they have been taught—weigh them and come to their own decision," said Connie Lawrence, a psychologist at the University of Bridgeport. She cited the famous Proverbs 22:6, but emphasized several key words: "Train a child in the way he should go, and when he is old he will not turn from it." She said the key here is a recognition that it will take time, plus trial and error. The Prodigal Son had to find out for himself that he was on the wrong path. "Set the teenager free to become his own person. Have faith in God and in him."

Her most important advice, however, was one word: "Listen—especially when you don't agree, listen. Afterwards, you can express your disagreement. The most frequent complaint I hear is 'My parents don't care about me. They don't listen to me.'"

Wilson Alling, a teacher at Greenwich Country Day School, suggested that one way to teach values is through "shared reading." Pin provocative articles on your teenager's door, and ask for their reaction to them. That makes conversation on tough subjects easier to start. More important, a parent should perceive that he or she is a role model who must live the values that he is trying to teach. And, he said, one must not only be honest, but also point out the opportunity to live dishonestly, and the reasons why one is honest.

"Kids are sensitive to hypocrisy," said Susan Payson, a staff member of FOCUS who works with a number of different private schools in eastern New England. "Therefore parents must be willing to admit failure. And when kids make the wrong choice, parents must avoid saying, 'I told you!'"

Unlike most kids, Susan likes to get to bed early and get up early. But the teens typically call in the middle of the night. "We have to make ourselves available—even when it is inconvenient," she says. And typically, Susan mostly listens, perhaps not saying more than five sentences. "That allows them to work through the problem on their own, and come to their own decision." (OK, parents, when was the last time you did that?)

Rev. Phil Lyman, a graduate of Princeton and, like Moore, an Episcopal clergyman, noted that after God gave Moses the Ten Commandments, he said, "These commandments that I give you today are to be upon your hearts. Impress them on your children. Talk about them when you sit at home and when you walk along the road, when you lie down and when you get up" (Deuteronomy 6:6-7).

Lyman adds, "God will hold you responsible or accountable for what you teach your children." But many parents leave Scripture teaching to their church's Sunday school. Instead, they allow their kids to spend hours every day in front of the TV. The obvious message is that too many parents don't really care enough about their values to teach them to their children. In addition to teaching them verbally, he says, "You must walk your talk. And when you fail, admit you were wrong."

The biggest trap many parents seem to fall into is "subjectivism," such as the father who made no protest when his son said he was taking a girl away for a weekend to the beach. "What can I do?" the father asks. "Kids have different values today."

"Clearly, to him, *right* and *wrong* are written with small letters," said Lyman. "Tell your children exactly what you think is right and wrong. Do it with sympathy and with stories that make your point. Jesus always taught with stories, which made abstract points memorable," said Lyman, who once was on the FOCUS staff in New England.

FOCUS's primary mission is to reach kids in prep school. But my own public school kids have gotten so much from men like Phil Lyman. "They don't assume you are a Christian," says my son John. All of us can learn from that approach.

A   n   s   w   e   r **4**

Campus Life Guides
Teens through Adolescence

I attended a baptism at a church in New York City. At one point, the pastor asked the congregation as a whole if they would assume responsibility to teach the child "all the things which a Christian ought to know and believe to his soul's health."

The congregation replied, rather ritually, "We will."

Really? What is your church doing to help teenagers discover Christ? Probably no more than what it is doing to help parents of teenagers cope! Having been the father of three teenage boys, I can testify that it's not only the kids who need help in navigating through the tumultuous waters of adolescence.

However, there is one regular source of hope, information, and tangible help: *Campus Life* magazine, published by the same company that produces *Christianity Today.*

My favorite column is written by Tim Stafford, who began his career at the magazine at age twenty-four. It is called "Love, Sex, and the Whole

Person" and is written in answer to letters sent in by kids.

"I am eleven years old going on twelve. I feel very ashamed of what I have done, and I've asked God and Jesus to forgive me. You see, I have had sex about five or six times with my brother. . . . It just feels so good! I can't stop! Would it be all right to keep doing it until I get mature enough?"

Stafford wrote back, "I can't find words strong enough to urge you to talk to someone—your mom, a pastor, a counselor, a Campus Life or Young Life leader or any adult Christian friend. You must find ways to stop having sex with your brother or anyone else, and you're going to need help to do that. These experiences, which simply feel so great to you now, can leave deep and damaging emotional wounds."

A few months later, a forty-eight-year-old woman wrote in to say that she was still suffering the "consequences of 'brotherly incest.'" As a teenager she "made out" with almost all boyfriends, and now rarely has sex with her husband because "I can't equate sex with love." She urged Tim to tell the eleven-year-old that the "good feelings will turn rotten over the years. She must stop *now*, and find help."

A more typical letter came from a sophomore at Arizona State who has fallen in love and is "faced with the temptation of having sex. . . . What can we do to keep from giving in?"

"I have not discovered a magical secret for resisting temptation," said Stafford. "What has helped

many people is a simple, old-fashioned goal: I want
to save myself for marriage." However, he goes on
to say that the "rare" person who enters marriage
"completely open, vulnerable, inexperienced and
uncalloused" has much to gain. "A relationship
never stands still. It either grows stronger or it begins
to fade. Sex may seem to be the easiest medicine for
a fading relationship, but it usually only makes matters worse. Sex definitely adds interest and it seems
to communicate deep love. But it won't strengthen
relationships. I've never known a couple who broke
up because they didn't go far enough. I've known
many who broke up because sexual attraction eventually dominated the relationship."

A major 1991 study by the U.S. Center for
Health statistics reports that those who have lost
their virginity before marriage *are 60 percent more
likely to divorce than those who marry as virgins.* So
Stafford gives practical tips on handling sexual
temptation. "Talk not only about how far you will
go, but for how long. Set time limits. Make decisions now and enforce them with each other."

Campus Life is unusual in that it appeals to both
high school and college kids, to males and females,
and is read by 80 percent of parents as well as kids!
Why? Consider the range of topics in one issue:

1. Overcoming stress: an article that includes a
twenty-five-question test that enables students to
measure how serious stress is in their lives, gives
forty examples of how "not to cope," along with
fifteen positive suggestions. "Don't let things slide.
Indecision and procrastination eventually create

added stress. . . . Do something for someone else. It will get your mind off your own problems. . . . Do what is morally right."

2. Cheap dates for cheapskates: "Spread a blanket on top of a hill with a pretty view. Give yourselves an hour to write a poem for each other."

3. Spark: a regular feature "to help handle life's hassles," begins with a boy telling of how "grossed out" he was at the sight of blood or the prospect of pain. Then he was surprised by a dentist who drilled without Novocain, which hurt less than the shot. "Are there, perhaps, benefits to facing and enduring the pains of life?" the boy asks. The answers are totally scriptural in this feature. "Read Psalms 44 . . . James 1:2-8, 2 Corinthians 12:1-10." For an insight into Christ's pain "Read Isaiah 53."

And the issue has a fifty-four-page college guide section, packed with ads for sixty-eight Christian schools, an unbiased guide to them, and articles like "Surviving Freshman Year."

However, Tim Stafford's column is the best-read feature. In an interview, he told me "there is an incredible void of guidance" on sex. "Schools are intimidated. Parents are intimidated. And churches fall very easily into the trap of thinking Christian kids will fall into a Christian pattern. . . . But many kids are in deep pain."

To help, *Campus Life* has a "Leader's Guide" edition that every adult working with youth ought to read. In fact, many subscriptions are sold in bulk to church youth groups for as little as $1.25 per issue. Why doesn't your church give it a try? Or why not buy a subscription for $14.95 for a teen who you'd like to meet Christ? Write Campus Life, P.O. Box 11618, Des Moines, IA 50340, or phone 1-800-678-6083.

A   n   s   w   e   r 5

"Young Life" Gives Hope to Unchurched Teens

Many American teenagers are in trouble. Half are from broken homes and feel like throwaways. Even those exposed to religion have shocking values. A poll conducted in a Stamford, Connecticut, high school found that while 80 percent of kids attend church and pray, half believe it is not wrong to cheat in class or take illegal drugs, and 70 percent say intercourse is not wrong, even for those under sixteen. But there is a Christian answer in a program called Young Life.

The following is a true story of painful conflict between father and daughter. It is also one of love, spiritual rebirth, and hope. It happened when my former hometown of Stamford launched Young Life.

Debbie's mother left when she was three, prompting Tom, her father, to turn to alcohol. He hired Sara to care for his three children. She did such a good job that Tom married her. Sara helped him turn from alcohol to an active church life.

But when Sara had children of her own, severe conflict erupted with Debbie, now a teenager. Debbie skipped school, hung around drop-outs, came

home high on pot, or was out all night. Tom alter-
nately called her a slut or crazy and frequently
made her a prisoner at home.

Then Tom met Shawn Kuhn, staff member of
Young Life, a national organization based in Colorado (P.O. Box 5520, Colorado Springs, CO 80901)
that reaches out to unchurched high school students to bring to them the relevance of Christ.
Young Life adult volunteers who care about kids
meet them at games, etc., inviting them to attend
a weekly "club" meeting that features singing, fun
pie-in-the-face skits, and a brief talk on the gospel.
Over vacation breaks, they take teens on trips.

Two of the volunteers that Debbie related to
were Alex and Barbara McEwen, a young Catholic
couple. And she became friends with Sue, the
daughter of Mrs. O'Reilly, a member of the Stamford Young Life Committee, which oversees the
program.

"Mom, listen to the screaming at Debbie's
house," said Sue, holding the phone out. "She's
talking about running away from home."

Mrs. O'Reilly listened and said, "Debbie, why
don't you come spend the weekend with us?"

"If I go, Dad says I can't ever come home," she
replied in tears.

"Nonsense. I'll be there shortly."

Tom had reached the end of his rope. When
Debbie visited her mother in a distant city a year
earlier, he and Sara had discovered the joy of a
peaceful home. Now he felt the only way to break
Debbie's rebellion and to find tranquility was to

keep his sixteen-year-old out until she accepted his rules. "She'll have to hit bottom before she'll come crawling back," he was heard to say.

Tom refused to take Debbie back that Sunday night. Mrs. O'Reilly already had five children, but without hesitation, she invited Debbie into her home. She lived there three months. "For the first time in my life, I went to bed at night feeling happy," said Debbie. Hurt and embarrassed, Tom would not speak to Mrs. O'Reilly, whom he saw as giving Debbie a cushy refuge from reality. Shawn brought father and daughter together where he mediated a discussion about her future. They agreed she should go to Young Life camp for a week that summer at Saranac, New York, and to boarding school in the fall.

"Saranac blew my mind," recalls Debbie. "It was so much fun. And on the last day a volunteer took me out on a sailboat where he asked me if I had committed my life to the Lord. I replied, 'I don't have my life together yet. And I don't know the Bible.'"

"You don't have to know the Bible to make a decision about your life," he said. "Debbie, do you have two groups of friends?" She nodded. "Describe them, he said."

"One is a bunch of dropouts who hang around, drink, and smoke pot; they don't have much of a future. My other friends are at Young Life. I can have fun with them without getting high."

The volunteer explained, "Doesn't that make your choice easy? In committing your life to

Christ, you are simply choosing your Young Life friends over the others. You cannot stay on the fence."

But Debbie still hesitated, doubtful. "I am not sure I can avoid past mistakes in the future."

He replied, "If you accept Jesus and turn to him when you are tempted, he will always help."

Suddenly her choice was easy.

When Debbie returned, she stayed with the McEwens. "It was a deeply spiritual experience for us. She was so easy to love and so well-intentioned." In fact, the experience was so rewarding that they are open to having other teenagers come in their home if the need arises.

Debbie is happily immersed in boarding school now. The Young Life volunteers and her father have visited her. His wounds are beginning to heal. Debbie asked him if she could visit a friend's family in Boston. He checked with the headmaster and found that her grades and conduct had been good, so her dad said, "OK, you've earned my trust."

Her father told me, "This has been a very painful experience, but I can see the hand of the Lord in it, especially in the love that has been shown my daughter through Young Life."

6   A n s w e r

Children Need Their Fathers

"The irony of this Father's Day is that the United States is an increasingly fatherless society," said David Blankenhorn, president of the Institute of American Values, two days before Father's Day.

"Tonight more than a third of our nation's children will go to sleep in homes in which their fathers do not live. Before they reach age eighteen, more than half our nation's children will live apart from their fathers. Fatherlessness is now approaching a rough parity with fatherhood as a defining feature of American childhood. This is so disturbing that many people prefer to ignore it."

Correct. We speak euphemistically of "single parent homes," when over 80 percent of 10 million homes are moms and kids.

"Never before in our nation's history have so many children grown up without a father's presence and provision," said Blankenhorn. The result? "Fatherlessness is the engine that drives our most pressing social problems," he adds. "It's the most important predictor of juvenile crime—a greater predictor than either race or income." Five out of six prisoners in Hawaii have no father. Girls growing up in fatherless homes are nearly three times as likely to have an illegitimate child as those in intact families. Why?

Karl Zinsmeister, another speaker at a forum hosted by the Family Research Council, said fathers are uniquely able to help children "understand the requirements for living in the world outside the family." They nudge their kids to "explore the outer levels of their competence and withstand frustration, and are critical in the establishment of stronger sexual identity and character in both boys and girls."

If the father's absence is due to death, daughters

actually perform better—and as adults have a 65 percent better chance of having a successful marriage than a girl in an intact family, says the National Survey of Families and Households. But if there is no dad because of divorce, white daughters are almost twice as likely to have a broken marriage. Why?

"Contrary to popular belief, many children do not bounce back after divorce or remarriage," writes Barbara Dafoe Whitehead in an article examining the dissolution of two-parent families in the April 1993 edition of *Atlantic* magazine. "Children who grow up in single-parent or stepparent families are less successful as adults, particularly in the two domains of life—love and work—that are most essential to happiness."

The child of divorce feels worthless because of dad's abandonment. "Boys are generally harder hit," says Zinsmeister. "They tend to have trouble concentrating in school, to do poorly on intelligence tests, and have difficulty with math. Fatherlessness significantly increases the likelihood of a boy becoming violent." The fatherless boy is more likely to join a gang in a search for male authority and a sense of belonging. The most misogynistic (women-hating) males in America are those raised in inner-city matriarchies. All those rap anthems about raping and torturing women come out of a world wholly devoid of male presence."

Zinsmeister had two solid ideas. First, to instill male family virtues in inner cities where they are most absent, cities should develop "residential schools for boys and girls, and all-male public schools perhaps staffed by decommissioned military officers" who can build discipline, self-respect, and morale. But when Detroit and Milwaukee tried to create all-male schools, they were shot down by the National Organization for Women and the ACLU!

Second, he said, "we must make divorce less easy." How? He proposed a "two-track marriage system." One track would allow either partner to dissolve a marriage at will, today's "no fault" system. The other track would not allow divorce unless an existing spouse proved the partner was "at fault." Anyone wanting a lasting marriage would choose Plan B.

I have two other suggestions. Pastors must begin to teach what the Bible says about marriage, divorce, and sex outside marriage. I asked the editors of the nation's Southern Baptist newspapers if they had ever heard a sermon on cohabitation. Only one editor out of fifty raised her hand! Malachi 2:7-8 says that "the lips of a priest ought to preserve knowledge" and that God curses the blessings of pastors whose teaching has "caused many to stumble."

The law also needs to be made much tougher on deadbeat dads who do not provide child support. Of 10 million mothers with children, only half have court orders that absent fathers contribute. And of the 5 million who are supposed to get payments, half receive nothing or only partial payments. No wonder a third of abandoned mothers live in poverty.

One way hundreds of thousands of fathers escape prosecution or wage withholding is to move across state lines. "Dereliction of this duty robs American children of billions of dollars," says Illinois Representative Henry Hyde. He has proposed a law that deserves passage: a Child Support Recovery Act that would make "interstate flight to avoid payment of child support" a federal crime.

7   A   n   s   w   e   r

Communitarian Platform Seeks to Strengthen Families

Former vice president Dan Quayle touched a deep chord when he said, "Marriage is probably the best antipoverty program of all. Among families headed by married couples today, there is a poverty rate of 5.7 percent," while a third "of families headed by single mothers are poor."

That comment was lost in the flap on his comments about Murphy Brown. But Quayle did not mention a U.S. marriage dissolution rate of 60 percent. He implied the "failure of our families" is a ghetto issue, when it actually cuts across all classes. I think it is the central problem of domestic America. Each year a million kids see parents divorce and another million are born out of wedlock.

A far more comprehensive analysis can be seen in "The Communitarian Platform" published in November 1991 by some thoughtful liberals such as George Washington University professor Amitai

Etzioni and William Galston, deputy assistant to President Bill Clinton. Key conservatives have signed it too, such as Bryce Christensen of the Rockford Institute and Father Richard John Neuhaus, the president of Religion and Public Life Institute. The Communitarian approach appeals to conservatives because it calls for traditional family values and responsibilities accompanying rights, while liberals like its support of governmental help for families in need.

The Communitarian Platform thus forges a healthy, broad new consensus: No community can "long survive unless its members dedicate some of their attention, energy, and resources to shared projects. The exclusive pursuit of private interest erodes the network of social environments on which we all depend, and is destructive to . . . democratic self-government."

A communitarian perspective mandates a focus on "responsibilities that must be borne by citizens, individually and collectively."

"The best place to start is where each new generation acquires its moral anchoring: at home in the family. We must insist . . . that bringing children into the world entails a moral responsibility to provide, not only material necessities, but also moral education [which] is not a task" to "be delegated to baby-sitters or even professional child-care centers. It requires close bonding of the kind that is formed only with parents."

The platform supports paid and unpaid parental leave. But it also asserts, "Child-rearing is important, valuable work that must be honored rather than denigrated. Two-parent families are better able to discharge their child-raising duties if only because there are more hands—and voices available for the task. It follows that widespread divorce, when there are children involved . . . is indicative of a serious social problem.

"Though divorces are necessary in some situations, many are avoidable and are not in the interest of children, the community, and probably not of most adults either. Divorce laws should be modified." (Can you think of any religious denomination speaking so boldly?)

"Above all, we should cancel the message that divorce puts an end to responsibilities among members of a child-raising family." How? "Reform the economic aspects of divorce laws so that the enormous financial burden of marriage dissolution no longer falls primarily on minor children and those parents who are their principal caretakers. . . . The principle of 'children first' should be made fundamental" when courts grant divorces.

That's a remarkable statement, the likes of which I have not heard from any Protestant or Jewish denomination.

Why do United Methodists, Episcopalians, Presbyterians debate homosexuality ad nauseam and ignore such issues as marriage, divorce, and the need for two-parent families? Southern Baptists argue that the Bible is "inerrant," conveniently ignoring Malachi 2:16: "'I hate divorce,' says the Lord God of Israel."

By contrast, the National Conference of Catholic Bishops issued a "Children's Statement" that sounded "communitarian": "Families are undermined by parental irresponsibility *and* discrimination and poverty." Therefore the bishops called for "changed behavior *and* changed policies." They want tax cuts for families with children to encourage mothers to stay home to raise them, welfare reform promoting self-help, and changes in divorce law to put "children first," focusing on adequate property and income to meet the needs of the children and their custodial parent before disposing marital property, and tough new rules for establishing and collecting child support.

The Communitarian Platform should spark a similar rethinking of how to strengthen families in every denomination. For a copy, call 1-800-245-7460.

A   n   s   w   e   r 8

Focus on the Family
Gives Answers to Problems

Undoubtedly, the reason Ann Landers and Abigail Van Buren are American's most popular columnists is that they offer common-sense advice on the range of personal problems that people face. But they only publish a couple of letters a day.

What if you are facing serious problems right now—a marriage that seems headed toward the rocks, defiant children, a history of sexual abuse, or serious conflict with parents? To whom can you turn?

Every day twelve thousand people write to

Dr. James Dobson, a psychologist who is president of Focus on the Family, a Christian family ministry, located in Colorado Springs. Every letter is answered, without any fee being charged!

Dobson's first book, *Dare to Discipline* (Wheaton, Ill.: Tyndale, 1973) established him as a worthy successor to Dr. Spock. He said, for example, that no ten-month-old should "take complete charge of two mature adults and mold them to suit her fancy." His solution: "Strike a reasonable balance between giving your baby the attention she needs and establishing her as a tiny dictator. Don't be afraid to let her cry a reasonable period of time."

There have been many additional books, whose sales soared into the millions: *Hide or Seek, Preparing for Adolescence, Straight Talk to Men and Their Wives, Love Must Be Tough, What Wives Wish Their Husbands Knew about Women,* and others.

An amazing 70 million Americans have seen his film series entitled Focus on the Family. His daily radio program of the same name is broadcast on nearly two thousand radio stations—more than that of anyone except Paul Harvey.

Curiously, however, he is relatively unknown to the secular world because his radio show is mostly on religious stations. Yet no one gives more practical aid to more people than Focus on the Family. It mails out fifty thousand books and sixty thousand tape recordings each month.

More than a tenth of the letters ask for serious personal advice. Topics range from marital problems and questions on bringing up children to alcohol or drug abuse and depression. Since Dobson served on the attorney general's Commission on Pornography, thousands of letters have also come from sexually abused people and pornography addicts.

They are answered by a staff of sixty people headed by Dianne Passno, who was one of only five letter writers when she started in 1982. The staff draws on a file of answers two feet thick that Dr. Dobson has written for hundreds of questions. And, to the surprise of those seeking help, many are also sent an appropriate tape or book at no cost.

The most urgent letters will get a call from one of nine counselors directed by Patti Crail. "This is crisis counseling," she says. "The involvement is very quick, with the aim of bringing resources to solve a serious problem. Often we refer the person to a local licensed professional counselor. We try to make two calls an hour. But if we are handling an abuse case, in which the authorities need to become involved, a case could take a half a day."

The advice is so helpful that Focus on the Family received $78 million in donations in 1992 to help support its nonprofit work.

And only three hundred of the daily twelve thousand letters have any criticism of Dobson. More typically, a New Mexico woman said: "About two years ago, I wrote you because my husband and I were experiencing great feelings of anger toward our newborn daughter. A few days later, a member of your staff called to recommend we seek counseling. Thank you for having a caring, concerned staff who takes the time to help your listeners. If it hadn't been for that call, we might not have gotten the help we needed."

A woman in Kansas City was beaten for four years by her husband until she began to implement advice in Dobson's book *Love Must Be Tough* (Waco, Tex.: Word, 1983). Her relationship with her husband is now healed.

An adult incest victim in California whose father is an alcoholic was referred to a doctor who is helping her "to feel normal again." She wrote that "signs of healing of my emotions are already taking place."

A twenty-nine-year-old physician in Oregon was so distraught by the death of his wife in a car accident that he was neglecting his four-year-old son until he saw Dobson in a film series called "Turn Your Heart Toward Home," which can be rented from Focus on the Family.

After seeing it, the doctor wrote, "My first priority is no longer my self-pity or my career. It is my son. I don't know how to thank you. I truly believe if I had not seen your program, I could have lost my son."

An Alabama mother wrote, "Thank you so much for the books, tapes, and precious letters and phone calls that I have received from your staff since you learned of the death of my daughter. How I wish I could embrace you for having nurtured me in such a caring way."

If you are having family problems on which you need advice, write Dr. James Dobson, Focus on the Family, P.O. Box 35500, Colorado Springs, CO 80935-3550.

Protect Kids from Violence and Danger

One of the primary obligations of a parent is to protect our children from dangers, both external and internal.

Most parents think immediately of one external danger that gets a lot of publicity: the child molester. How can parents protect kids from sexual predators? Answer 9 gives information that most parents don't have. Do you know at what age a child is most likely to be seduced? Which sex is more at risk? How do molesters lure the children they ravish? Ken Wooden, a producer of ABC's "20/20," interviewed molesters in prison to find out whom they target and just how they operate. Wooden has produced a pamphlet every parent should read. Answer 9 tells how to get it.

Not all dangers, however, are external. The dangers most kids face are more insidious. They arise not from predators but from internal, media-fanned temptations. Some kids are so addicted to TV that every day they waste hours that could otherwise be invested in sports, music, or other healthy activities. What do they learn from watching all this TV?

Negative values. Kids think that to be successful, what matters are looks, sex, cars, and money. Some kids find violence attractive. "It has been estimated that by the time the average child reaches age eighteen, he will have witnessed more than 15,000 murders on television or in the movies," writes Dr. William Bennett in his "Index of Leading Cultural Indicators." "Research shows that children and even teenagers have a difficult time distinguishing between what is fiction and what is reality." He cites research that "heavy exposure to televised violence is one of the causes of aggressive behavior, crime, and violence in society."

And the younger the viewer, the more negative the impact of violence-drenched TV and films. Here is some indirect evidence from the Uniform Crime Reports: Between 1985 and 1991, there was a 20 percent increase in arrests of those age twenty-one to twenty-four for murder. But among those age eighteen to twenty, arrests for murder leapt 113 percent; for seventeen year olds it jumped 121 percent; for sixteen year olds, arrests soared 158 percent; and among fifteen year olds, arrests sky-rocketed 217 percent—ten times the growth rate of those age twenty-one to twenty-four who watch much less TV.

Americans are watching TV two hours more per day than they did three decades ago—more than seven hours a day now. Dr. Bennett cites a 1991 survey in which only 2 percent of respondents indicated that they thought television should have the greatest influence on children's values, "but 56

percent believe that it has the greatest influence—
more than parents, teachers, and religious leaders
combined."

How can a parent protect a child from the
unhealthy temptations of our worldly society?
The task may seem impossible. However, there are
practical steps a parent can take.

Turn off the TV. Answer 10 provides evidence
from a thousand studies that kids learn from TV
that personal conflict is best resolved by violence.
Excessive TV watchers are 150 percent more likely
to be convicted of crime than light watchers. Half
of cartoons "glorify violence or use violence to
entertain," says the National Coalition on Television Violence. "Children who watch a heavy diet
of violence experience more nightmares and are
more fearful. Another major effect . . . is desensiti-
zation to the seriousness and cruelty of violence."

A 1993 report by the Coalition on Television
Violence says that 25 percent of prime-time TV is
so violent and potentially harmful that it ought to
begin with a warning: "This program is dangerous
to your health."

At our house the TV was *off* during the week.
That allowed our boys time to practice musical
instruments, study enough to achieve, and get
involved with sports, board games, pets, and so
forth. Our kids knew they could watch certain
wholesome shows on the weekends. Interestingly,
they never accused us of being unfair with our
strict TV rules.

You set the tone in your family. So why not turn off your TV?

Don't buy your child violent toys. Answer 11, originally written in 1987, noted that there were twenty-nine cartoons with war themes. Most were program-length commercials for toys such as HeMan, G.I. Joe, and Captain Power. I urged parents to protest by writing the Federal Communications Commission, asking that such programming end. Parents did write in, and G.I. Joe dolls are no longer sold on a G.I. Joe show. But G.I. Joe is still aired, and the dolls are still sold.

We never even bought our kids cap guns. Instead, we got a saxophone for one son, a violin for another, a clarinet for the third. Today, all play music. You do not have to buy your children violent toys, either. Resist the commercials.

Boycott sponsors of destructive television. Over the last decade, the American Family Association has created an effective way for parents to stand up and be heard. They head up a movement to boycott the sponsors of violent, indecent, or profane television shows. Called CLeaR-TV (Christian Leaders for Responsible Television), this movement is led by well over a thousand religious leaders of all faiths.

Volunteers monitor prime-time programming, counting actual incidents of violence, sex, and profanity. CLeaR-TV then singles out one or two sponsors with the highest level of negative programming. Answer 12 reports the success of

CLeaR-TV's boycott of Clorox and Mennen. Clorox sales fell so sharply that the company published an apology and moved its ads to wholesome programs. Though Mennen changed some of its policies, the company refused to admit it. Sales continued to plummet, and Mennen sold out to Colgate-Palmolive.

Don Wildmon of the American Family Association says that TV programming has gotten worse despite CLeaR-TV. "It is more graphic, more bold. In 1989 we saw a man and woman going to bed. In 1992 it shows them undressing and nude on top of each other." The struggle for decent TV continues. Learn how to add your consumer power to the fight.

Keep all pornography out of your home. If you have a son, you can bet he is into pornography at some level. Magazines, videos, and cable TV are easily available. You may not be able to keep him from ever seeing any pornographic material, but you can keep pornography out of your home.

Do not subscribe to HBO or other cable movie channels, which run movies late at night that show full nudity. Do not permit your son to subscribe to *Playboy*. If you find such a magazine in his room, throw it away. Explain the danger so he will not bring home another. Answer 13 provides evidence of the harm of even soft-core magazines, as reported by the *Final Report of the Attorney General's Commission on Pornography* (to which I wrote the forty-page introduction). Alaska has the highest rate of sales of such magazines; it also has the highest rape rates.

Even R-rated slasher movies will create a fetish in some boys that prevents them from becoming sexually aroused unless they see a woman raped or hurt. More commonly, men become addicted to pornography and prefer it to sex with their wives. Pornography is a factor in a surprising percent of divorces.

Don't let your kids drive at age sixteen. Sixteen-year-olds are three times as lethal behind the wheel as eighteen-year-olds. Half of those aged sixteen and seventeen will have at least one crash, according to a survey of students. Add a kid to your insurance policy and see the rates skyrocket. I presented those facts in the original version of Answer 14 in 1981, and my wife and I concluded that our sons would not drive until they were seventeen years old.

The second part of Answer 14 was written after eight successful years of imposing that discipline. My boys hated it, but they survived. My wife and I had to chauffeur them around longer, but that was a price we were willing to pay. Our rule no doubt prevented some wrecks. In addition it postponed for a year the handing over of a portable motel room. It stretched out their adolescence and gave us peace of mind.

9 A n s w e r

Children Can Learn How to Protect Themselves against Molesters

If you want to warn children in your family, school, or church about how to protect themselves against child molesters, you must be informed.

Take out a pencil and test how much you know with these questions:

1. Which age group is the prime target of the child molester/abductor?
A. 6–8 years   B. 10–12 years   C. 14–16 years
2. Which sex is more likely to be approached by a molester/abductor?
A. Female   B. Male   C. Even percentage
3. Of the following lures, which is most often used by the molester/abductor?
A. Picture taking   B. Asking for help   C. Bribe
D. Force
4. What percent of the molester/abductor suspects are nonwhite?
A. 45 percent   B. 30 percent   C. 15 percent
D. 1 percent

If you did not take the test, don't read further. I'm willing to guess that you will flunk it. I confess that I got all of these questions wrong!

In 1977, Oakland County, Michigan, police were trying to solve seven child murders, four believed to be by the same person. With an interview guide, some 782 previously unreported cases of molestation surfaced in the fourth through ninth grades in fifty-four schools. The test above is based on those interviews. The answers:

1. Molesters prefer the ten- to twelve-year old group five to ten times more than the other ages because they most like kids on the brink of puberty.

2. Surprisingly, 49 percent of cases involve boys!

Yet girls are four times as likely to report incidents. Why? Boys fear parental restriction.

3. "Don't take candy from the stranger" is the advice parents give kids. Abductors know that, so only 3 percent offer bribes. But 29 percent ask kids for directions. Only 4 percent use coercion. Most of the molesters are people known to the children. One study says that 12 percent of stepfathers molest their daughters!

4. Only one percent of cases were by blacks.

And there are hundreds of cases involving Catholic priests. About $400 million in negligence payments for damages were paid by 1992, enough to halt church insurance coverage. Several hundred million dollars of law suits are pending. Bankruptcy is possible. Yet Mark Chopko, general counsel of the National Conference of Catholic Bishops, could cite no clear guidelines for bishops in handling such cases, or any recommended program to help children avoid molesters.

Fortunately, there is a superb pamphlet, "Child Lures Family Guide," requested by one million people to educate kids on self-protection. It was written by Ken Wooden and was first made available during an ABC News "20/20" show he produced, "The Lures of Death." "I went to the 'experts'—child molesters and murderers," he says, "to find out how they lured children so that I could educate parents."

Fred Fetterolf, president of Alcoa, was so impressed with it, he sent the guide to his fifty thousand employees, saying, "Criminal acts

against children for the sexual and avaricious grati-
fication of adults are carried out with surprising
ease. . . . They know exactly what appeals to children and are cunning in their offense. We must be
as clever in our defense. I'm sending you this book-
let in hope that you will read it as a family and be
sure your children understand how to protect
themselves." It has also been endorsed by the
Knights of Columbus and New York City police.

In addition, Wooden has prepared a curriculum
and two videotapes—one to train educators, pastors, health workers, and police, and the other for
kids. In them, he shows how to teach "without
scaring" children.

Seated in front of a desk, the bearded, fiftyish
producer first asks some kids, "What is a lure?"
A precocious child says, "It's to coax you out of
safety." The producer replies, "Yes, like bait when
you go fishing." Examples:

1. Affection—Children have been told to be
wary of strangers, but are caught off guard when
relatives or friends are inappropriately intimate.
"There is good love and bad love," he says, holding up fake money and real cash. "Know the difference." Wooden holds up bathing suits and says, "If
someone puts his hand down your bathing suit, is
that real love or bad love?" They shouted, *"Bad!"*

2. Assistance—Two boys are asked to come forward, are shown a puppy leash, and asked whether
they'd help a man find a lost puppy. They nodded
yes. Two girls also said they'd help a man pick up
fallen packages. Others said they'd give directions

to someone who asked. "These are clever tricks," Wooden says, grabbing a boy to demonstrate. "If asked directions, take two giant steps back and be ready to run like the wind."

3. Authority—"Some people make believe they are a priest, doctor, or policeman. They can show a badge like this, and say, 'You have been shoplifting. Come with me.' What would you do? Look to see if the name of your town is on the badge. Call the police and ask if he works for them."

4. Ego—"Someone might say, 'How would you like to be a model on TV? You'll make five hundred dollars each time an ad is shown. But don't tell your mom and dad.'"

Every family, every church, every school has a moral obligation to help kids avoid lures of death. To learn more, write Wooden Publishing House, 2119 Shelburn Road, Shelburn, VT 05482.

10 A n s w e r

NCTV Fights Violence on Television

Note: While this column is a few years old, the excess of violence on television is still a problem. Please note that companies mentioned here as targeted for boycotts may have been taken off boycott lists. Please write NCTV for a current list of promoters of violence.

Recently, my wife asked, "Have you noticed that young children seem more violent than they were when our kids were small [twenty years ago]?"

She's right. We've always owned basset hounds, extraordinarily gentle dogs who love to play with children. Even toddlers never had to fear a bite from this gentle breed even though they might fall right on top of one. Our dogs were neighborhood favorites.

Boys aged five to eight still love to play with Bones, our newest basset. But they are apt to poke him with sticks, with plastic swords bought by their parents, and to have him jump so they can push him back making his head hit the driveway. They all laugh at their cruelty. This is unprecedented.

But what are kids' favorite TV programs? Shows such as "Freddy's Nightmares," with fourteen to twenty-eight violent acts per hour, says the National Coalition on Television Violence. It adds, "Five of seven episodes of 'Freddy's Nightmares' included persons killed by members of their own family." Freddy used his razor-blade fingers to put out one person's eyes and slashed the throat of another in one show.

A favorite movie of kids is *Friday the 13th,* with thirty-two to fifty-six violent acts per hour. And what violence! A teenage girl escaping from a gang rape is hit by a car and crippled. "A satanic wheelchair allows her to recover gradually by killing her attackers one by one. She makes sexual advances on one boy, ties him down, and electrocutes him," said NCTV.

One study asked preteens (ages ten to twelve) to identify famous people. Jason of *Friday the 13th* and Freddy were correctly identified by 80 percent of kids. George Washington was known by 70 percent; Lincoln, 36 percent.

What's the evidence such shows are harmful? Over one thousand research studies have documented the harm. The U.S. Surgeon General's task force on violence said evidence is "overwhelming" that violent entertainment has a harmful effect. For example, a twenty-two-year study that began with middle class third graders in 1960 found that a quarter of kids with the heaviest diet of violent TV were actually convicted of crime 150 percent more often than those with lightest viewing! And a diet of heavy viewing was the best predictor of convictions as a juvenile delinquent.

NCTV Chairman Dr. Thomas Radecki, a psychiatrist, charges that "our national diet of cruel, violent entertainment" has even made America more militaristic. "The U.S. spends more money per capita on the military than any other country in the world; 25 percent of all government expenditures. . . . No other Western democracy spends more than 10 percent. Our nation also has the highest levels of violence" on TV and films. He cites research: Dr. George Gerbner of the University of Pennsylvania found that "as the number of hours of TV viewing increased for middle class adults, their support for military expenditures and opposition to nonmilitary foreign aid increased." (Such viewers are also more likely to fear walking in their own neighborhood at night and to own handguns.)

Radecki says, "The idea that international conflicts are best resolved by violent actions or threats is an extension of the thinking that personal conflicts are best resolved in this manner," yet violence is the content of 30 percent of prime-time shows.

But there are some signs of hope. Many readers of Dr. Radecki's "NCTV News" have written advertisers of the most violent shows (as have members of Don Wildmon's American Family Association). And the message is beginning to get through.

First, "The levels of violence on Saturday morning cartoons are at their lowest level in over a decade," says NCTV. Gone are the superheroes like The Incredible Hulk, Spiderman, and G.I. Joe. But cartoons on ABC still have twenty-four acts of violence per hour versus CBS and NBC with seventeen per hour.

Second, "For the fourth year in a row, TV violence is down in the Neilsen ratings and somewhat down in quantity." "Miami Vice" and "The Equalizer," two of the most violent shows, have finally been taken off the air.

Third, 80 percent of the advertisers on the extremely violent and sadistic "Freddy" and "Friday" shows have dropped their sponsorships or promised NCTV they will do so. However, one of the remaining advertisers is the U.S. Army. Your tax dollar is thus promoting violence among kids!

If that makes you furious, write your member of Congress. NCTV wants you to boycott other sponsors: Nabisco, Coors, Burger King, and Nintendo.

Nintendo is a new form of killing for kids. Radecki calls it "a game of nonstop violence." It allows kids to use their TV screen to kill their opponents. Of American's twenty best-selling toys, twelve are Nintendo games. Sadly, Nintendo, like the TV shows it sponsors, is not harmless.

To help fight violence on TV, send $25 to be a member of NCTV, P.O. Box 2157, Champaign, IL 61825.

11 A n s w e r

Violent Toys Increase Aggression in Children

Are your youngest children more violent than older siblings? Perhaps you can thank the Federal Communications Commission for its deregulation of children's television.

In 1969, Mattel sponsored a cartoon called "Hot Wheels," which was the same name as a plastic tricycle Mattel manufactured. The FCC ruled the cartoon was, in effect, a program-length commercial that violated the Communications Act, and banned the practice. Why? Children can't tell the difference between ads and the program.

This wise rule was changed in 1983, again under Mattel's initiative for the "HeMan" cartoon and toy combination. And what is the result of this so-called "deregulation?"

In 1984, HeMan sales hit the roof, and a new toy from Japan, Voltron, was the fourth top-selling toy in America. In 1985 there were ten program-length commercials with war themes, and most were aired five days a week.

"In 1986, there were twenty-nine programs with war themes, and a dozen others selling other lines of toys," according to Thomas E. Radecki, research director of the National Coalition on Television Violence. The result was a "700 percent increase in the sales of war toys, totaling $1.3 billion last year."

"These toys are harmful because of the violent messages being sold. In dealing with conflict, they dehumanize the opponent—making him into an irredeemable evil character who can only be dealt with by force," Dr. Radecki said.

Further, the violence gets worse each year. Initially, the coalition counted only twenty-one acts of violence with the "HeMan" show in an hour. The average jumped to thirty-six violent acts in the 1985 shows, and to forty-eight in 1986. One show hit an incredible 130 acts of violence per hour— "Captain Power and Soldiers of the Future" with an attempted murder every thirty seconds and a killing once a minute. "The so-called 'forces of good' have averaged 61 percent killing efficiency, but the 'forces of evil' have a zero percent killing efficiency," says the coalition.

"Violence is repeatedly shown as the best and only way to deal with an enemy." And it is interactive, with viewers shooting at the screen. Light from the television screen interacts with a computer chip in fighter planes held by kids who are trying to kill bad guys with glowing emblems.

If they hit the villains, their planes emit a particular sound. A miss has a different sound. If the bad guys hit the fighter planes five times, a man pops out of the plane and falls on the floor. The weapon goes dead—but for only fifteen seconds. At one point "Captain Power" had a 3.3 Neilsen rating, which means 8 million children were watching it each week. At that time, the fighter plane was the eighth best-selling toy.

These programs have a powerful, measurable, negative impact. The National Coalition on Television Violence studied preschool children and second- and fourth-graders, some of whom watched the Captain Power show, and some of whom played with construction toys. On different days, the groups switched activities.

"On the Captain Power days, the children showed increases in playground aggression, averaging 80 percent more hitting, kicking, hair pulling, and sitting on top of another child than on the control days." But in two classrooms, the kids "showed a decrease in aggressiveness after playing cooperatively with construction toys."

These results are similar to other research that was done with HeMan, Transformers, Star Wars, and others. In general, harmful aggressiveness doubled among children watching these programs. Dr. Radecki, a psychiatrist in Champaign, Illinois, says categorically, "These war toys and their TV programs are teaching violence to our children and to children around the world."

Campaigns by groups like his coalition do have an impact. Coleco Industries in Hartford stopped making Rambo lines of toys because sales fell off after publicity urging parents not to buy them. But then it simply invented new ones—Star Com, about war in space, and Blast Force Power Cycle, a tricycle complete with a submachine gun.

Some four hundred groups in America and twenty-seven other countries have protested. The Alliance for Survival staged a "War Toys Steam Rolling," in which a five-ton steamroller crushed piles of toys into a peace symbol.

Veterans for Life in Minneapolis sells a poster, "Ask a soldier who knows the pain. Perhaps he'll tell you now. Guns are not toys. War is not a game." More important, Action for Children's Television has gotten federal courts to order the FCC to review deregulation of children's television.

I urge you to take three steps. First, don't let your children watch violent television. Second, do not put violent toys under a Christmas tree; they do not honor the Prince of Peace. Third, write the FCC at 1919 M Street NW, Washington D.C., protesting program-length commercials.

A   n   s   w   e   r *12*

Boycott of Sponsors Succeeds

I once wrote, "Are you sick of excessive sex, violence and profanity on television? Finally, there is something you can do. For the next year, boycott all products made by Clorox—Formula 409, Fresh Scent, Tilex, Liquid Plummer—and those of Mennen—Speed Stick, Skin Bracer, Afta."

Why? "Christian Leaders for Responsible Television (CLeaR-TV)—sixteen hundred leaders . . . the heads of seventy denominations and one hundred Catholic bishops—called for the boycott after monitoring by three thousand volunteers showed that Mennen and Clorox 'were among the leading sponsors of sex, violence and profanity.'"

That boycott was stunningly successful at two levels:

First, both companies slashed their ads on shows with sex, profanity, and violence. Clorox cut them by two-thirds, and Mennen "pulled out almost totally," says Dr. Billy Melvin, chairman of CLeaR-TV and executive director of the National Association of Evangelicals.

More important, there was an overall 32 percent drop in sex, violence, and profanity on all prime-time shows between spring 1989 and fall 1989. "That to me is the success of the boycott," says Melvin. An average hour of prime time registered thirty-four incidents on CBS, NBC, and ABC combined in the spring. The number fell to twenty-three incidents in November.

A key reason is that the networks dropped "Miami Vice," in which two heroes killed forty-three people in eighteen shows—five times what the real Miami police force killed in a year—and similar programs, such as "The Equalizer."

"It shows the power of the pocketbook," says Rev. Don Wildmon, the Methodist preacher who has brilliantly engineered CLeaR-TV's strategy. "You can cry, plead, and beg till you are blue in the face. Many advertisers will ignore you. But when you talk money, they listen. We sent out 23 million boycott cards (listing the products of each firm): 17.5 million to 175,000 churches, 3.5

million by direct mail and 2.5 million in response to orders that were paid for," Wildmon added.

"Those are imposing numbers, awesome numbers," said Joseph Smith, president of Oxtoby-Smith, a consumer research firm with many blue chip clients. "That is a very large number of consumers to be in communication with. What makes them imposing is that these are consumers presumably disposed to the message." But he added that the issue in New York "has virtually disappeared from prominent attention. I encounter no references to it." But he is not surprised with CLeaR-TV's impact. His independent research last year "found an extremely high proportion of people who found material on TV which was objectionable. Two-thirds objected to violence, gratuitous sex, and profanity." And he said viewers want "to do something about it."

They are not only going after Mennen and Clorox, but other companies cited in Wildmon's superb *AFA Journal,* published by his American Family Association. It describes some of the sleazy shows aired recently and cites the corporate sponsors, with names of top officers and addresses.

For example, General Motors was a sponsor of a "Doctor, Doctor" sitcom which "relies primarily on illicit and perverted sex jokes for its 'plot' development. The January 15, 1990, episode catalogued a bestiality joke, a male genital joke, and excretory joke, a sex doll joke, and an illicit sex joke."

GM also sponsored the movie *Pair of Aces,* which identified Christians "whose behavior represents everything but Christian principles," said AFA. A man leading a country church has an illicit lover and tells one man to "take that d——n hat off in church." Bubba, a teenage "Christian" football star says angels of God told him to murder six teenage girls.

"Literally thousands of letters" objecting to the shows have come to GM's chairman, according to John McNulty, vice president for public relations. And they sparked a result. "We have had a change in our screening policy," he said, "which we expect will eliminate further instances of GM commercials appearing on programs that don't meet our corporate guidelines," to keep out of programs that involve "gratuitous sex, or violence, or anything that reflects badly" on some people, such as Christians.

In the past, each division, such as Chevrolet, had programs screened by its own ad agencies. Now GM does all the screening in Detroit.

Thus, the progress is made, step by step when consumers register their opinions. CLeaR-TV picks new corporate targets on a regular basis. Watch denominational publications, or subscribe to the *AFA Journal* for $15 a year, P.O. Drawer 2440, Tupelo, MS 38803.

13 A n s w e r

Porn Is More Harmful than Many Believe

"The incest started at the age of eight. I did not understand any of it and did not feel that it was right," says Lydia S. on page 786 of the *Final Report of the Attorney General's Commission on Pornography.* "My dad would try to convince me that it was OK. He would find magazines with articles and/or pictures that would show fathers and daughters. . . . He would say that if it was published in magazines that it had to be all right because magazines could not publish lies."

A former prostitute is quoted on page 831: "We were all introduced to prostitution through pornography. There were no exceptions in our group, and we were all under eighteen. Pornography was our textbook. We learned the tricks of the trade by men exposing us to pornography and us trying to mimic what we saw."

With some exceptions, churches are shockingly mute on the plague of porn. Thousands of pastors speak out on the evil of abortion, but not on the evil of porn that often sparked the sex that led to abortion. I'm reminded of Malachi: "'And now this admonition is for you, O priests. If you do not listen . . .' says the Lord Almighty. . . . 'I will curse your blessings. . . . For the lips of a priest ought to preserve knowledge, and from his mouth men should seek instruction—because he is the messenger of the Lord Almighty. But you have turned from the way and by your teaching have caused many to stumble'" (Malachi 2:1-2, 7-8).

Perhaps the reason for the silence of so many pastors in the face of porn's evil is ignorance. Many honestly are unaware of how much of porn is mixed with violence or degradation—or how it causes violence. With the publication of the Pornography commission's report, ignorance is no longer an excuse.

A 1970 Presidential Commission on Obscenity "found no evidence" that explicit sexual material causes crime. That's "starkly obsolete," said the 1986 report. Why? Porn is now much more violent, and rape rates have doubled from 1970–1983, while other violent crimes have remained stable.

Some porn is now "sado-masochistic," with "whips, chains, [and] devices of torture." Another type of porn is graphic rape in which the victim resists, but "eventually becomes aroused and ecstatic . . . begging for more." Slasher films contain "suggestive nudity coupled with extreme violence." In *Toolbox Murders,* a nude woman in a tub is killed with a power drill.

Thus, the report's social science appendix concludes: "Circulation of materials which themselves portray sexual violence is a probable 'cause' of rape," a thesis that "73 percent of Americans accept as true."

The evidence cited ranges from victim testimony such as that above, to correlational, cross-cultural, and test data. The 1970 Commission was impressed by a Danish study which seemed to indicate a decrease in sex crimes after porn was deregulated. Its author has since "been forced to concede" that there were *"increases* in reports of rape." Even nonviolent, soft-core porn may justify rape. One study showed a "strong statistical relationship" between sales of the largest eight porn magazines and rape rates. Alaska's sales are five times higher per capita than North Dakota, and Alaska's rapes are sixfold higher!

While some dismiss this as "correlational," not evidence of proof, the commission notes that the surgeon general used similar correlational data to prove that those who smoke have "higher death and illness rates."

"Well over half" of sex offenders admit using adult men's magazines to increase "their deviant sexual interests." Rapists were fifteen times as likely as nonoffenders to have been exposed to 'hard core' porn as children aged six to ten. And they had earlier exposure to "bestiality, group sex, and sex activities with whips, belts or ropes." Police "consistently stated" that pornography is "routinely found on the person of or in the residence of arrested rapists." Even "normal" men are affected. College males who viewed six hours of nonviolent porn over six weeks "tend to increase callousness toward women and acceptance of 'rape myths' . . . trivializing rape" and its trauma.

Reading excerpts like this from a massive report is not enough for you to understand the depth and breadth of this problem. You must dip into the seventy pages of heart-rending victim testimony, 176 pages on how organized crime controls porn, 142 pages on child porn, etc.

But the report sold out though the government sold it for thirty-five dollars! I then arranged for it to be published by Rutledge Hill Press for $9.95 a copy. To get a copy, write to Rutledge Hill Press, 211 7th Ave. North, Nashville, TN 37219.

The Church of the Nazarene gave its five thousand pastors a copy, says Dr. B. Edgar Johnson, former head of the denomination. "They need to read the report themselves so they will be stirred to insist that obscenity laws are enforced by the authorities at local, state, and federal levels."

14 A n s w e r

Sixteen-year-olds Should Not Drive

Suppose your sixteen- or seventeen-year-old came home one day and said, "Kids at school are playing an exciting game, and I want to play it, too. It's a modified form of Russian roulette. But only one kid in a thousand dies and only one in five has a serious accident. OK?" Would you let him "play"? Before you say no, consider the name of this "game." It's called driving a car under age eighteen.

But to a teenager, nothing is more important than getting the driver's license. It is a key to freedom—from parents and to discover the opposite sex. All too often, it is also a key to falling grades, injury, and death.

As most people know, car accidents are the largest killer of those aged sixteen to twenty-four. What is not known is that access to a car is the reason hundreds of thousands of students drop out of high school. That was proven, in an odd way, in West Virginia. The legislature passed a law in 1988 that lifts the driver's license of any student who chooses to drop out of school. Result: the dropout rate was slashed by one-third! Normally, 5,000 West Virginia kids a year drop out of school—usually after they get "wheels." But by the time June 1989 rolled around, only 3,400 students had dropped out.

Yale professor Leon Robertson produced evidence that the major reason kids drive at that age is peer pressure combined with official state and local government encouragement through the provision of driver education. "If you're a teenager and you don't have wheels, you don't have anything," said Michelle Lee Fowler, a seventeen-year-old interviewed by *The New York Times*. She dropped out of Charleston's Stonewall Jackson High School but came back three months later when she learned she would lose her driver's permit. "That got my attention," she said.

More important, her attitude changed. "I was just bored and didn't care about school. Now I'll graduate. Maybe I'll try to go to college."

In other words, she thrived under the limits that impinged upon her freedom. The problem has been that we adults have done a very poor job of imposing any limits—such as taking the keys away from dropouts. Our leniency is partly responsible for a million teen pregnancies and for too many highway deaths involving teens: 3,326 for those aged sixteen and seventeen. Furthermore, while this age group represents only 3 percent of licensed drivers, it accounts for 10 percent of all deaths on the highway. So you and I are also in danger of being struck by them.

On this subject, my sons see me as a grump. None of them (now ages twenty-seven, twenty-four, and twenty-two) was sixteen when driver's licenses were permitted in our household. Each had to be seventeen. Why? I told them, "The odds are one in three you will have a serious accident during ages sixteen and seventeen. By eliminating one year of driving, the odds are cut in half. And that means insurance premiums are less." Other reasons: the temptations to drink and drive and to be sexually involved at too early an age are postponed till teens are more mature.

Why does any sixteen-year-old "have" to drive? The best answer they come up with is "to get a job." But the job just pays for the car. The real reason is that we parents are tired of driving them around.

The Insurance Institute for Highway Safety (IIHS) conducted a survey of fifty thousand male high school students a few years ago and found that nearly *half* with licenses for two years said that "they had had at least one crash." Half also reported getting one or more tickets for moving violations.

And nearly half of licensed male drivers said they had driven after drinking, and 25 percent do so *every week* or more often.

Another IIHS study by Dr. Leon Robertson of Yale concluded, "High school driver education produces a net harmful effect because it leads to increased numbers of licensed teenagers, which, in turn, increases the total crashes for that age group. A study of the experience of twenty-seven states for several years found that driver's education did not reduce the number of fatal crashes per ten thousand licensed sixteen- and seventeen-year-old drivers in a state."

However, states with higher percentages of teens taking driver's ed had more licensed drivers of that age, and more fatal crashes with them. Conversely, when Connecticut eliminated driver's ed from state funding, eight cities such as Norwalk and Waterbury dropped it from the curriculum.

The result was that 9,400 fewer students took driver's ed, and 7,680 fewer teens got their driver's licenses. And in those towns "the reported crashes per overall sixteen- and seventeen-year-old population . . . decreased by 63 percent from 1975–1978, compared to no change in communities that retained the course."

These are astounding findings that should prompt state legislators, schools, and parents to rethink conventional wisdom at three levels:

1. High school driver's training programs should be eliminated.
2. The age for a driver's license should be raised to seventeen.
3. Any high school dropout should lose his license till age eighteen.

And until states will legislate against young drivers, it's up to us parents to play the bad guys (or should I say "good guys") and do what is best for our children—don't let them drive at sixteen.

Fight Teenage Substance Abuse

So many children and teenagers have succumbed to the lures of tobacco, alcohol, street drugs, prescription drugs, and even household products such as glue and aerosol propellants, that a term was coined to cover the whole range of physical, mental, and emotional damage: *substance abuse*. What a lot of parents don't realize is the central role tobacco plays in the sad scenario.

Tobacco

Tobacco is a *gateway drug*—the first drug many children use as a stepping stone to experimentation with illicit drugs or heavy drinking. Kids who smoke are *six times as likely as nonsmokers* to experiment with cocaine and three times as likely to get drunk, according to the U. S. Institute on Drug Abuse.

The chart in this chapter shows that of high school seniors who smoke half a pack or more of cigarettes a day, 62 percent are involved in binge drinking and 50 percent have tried illicit drugs. Of high school seniors who do not smoke, only 19 percent drink heavily and 8 percent have tried illicit drugs.

Smoking and Drug Use
among High School Seniors, 1991

Percentage of high school seniors who smoked half a pack or more of cigarettes per day and used drugs within the past 30 days

Within the past 30 days . . .	Smokers	Non-smokers
Used any illicit drugs*	50%	8%
Used cocaine	6%	<1%
Drank alcohol	84%	42%
Binged**	62%	19%
Used marijuana	46%	6%

Note: 10 percent of seniors smoked half a pack of cigarettes or more per day in 1991.

* Illicit Drugs: includes any use of marijuana, hallucinogens, cocaine, and heroin, or any use of other opiates, stimulants, barbiturates, methaqualone, or tranquilizers not under a doctor's order.

** Binge drinking: five or more drinks in a row one or more times within the two weeks prior to the survey.

Source: Based on information supplied by the U.S. National Institute on Drug Abuse, Senior High School Survey 1991

From a parent's point of view, then, the highest priority in fighting *all* teenage substance abuse is to thwart any attempt by a son or daughter to smoke. Answer 15 suggests a creative way of educating children early on about the dangers of smoking. At what age is the danger greatest? Junior high or earlier! Most smokers begin their habit between ages ten and thirteen.

Are you surprised? Answer 16 quotes former Surgeon General C. Everett Koop as stating that 60

percent of smokers begin at age thirteen or younger. This column points to the orchestrated strategy of tobacco firms to sell their products to kids.
One result: a fifth of Arkansas *kindergartners* use
smokeless tobacco! How do they hear about it? It's
not hard to come by. Free samples are available at
rock concerts and at spitting contests held at fairs.

More recently, RJR Nabisco has been marketing
Camel cigarettes with a cartoon character named
Camel Joe. Do you have a six-year-old? Ask the child
who Camel Joe is. An astonishing 90 percent of kids
that young know Camel Joe is selling cigarettes.
And how successful is this cartoon character whose
face intentionally resembles male genitalia? "RJR
Nabisco's illegal sales of Camel cigarettes to minors
increased from about $6 million in 1987 to $476 million in 1990," says the *Tobacco Youth Reporter*.

Tobacco is a dangerous drug, even though it is
legally available to adults. In 1988 it was responsible for 434,000 deaths, according to the surgeon
general, and that estimate may be low. On Washington state death certificates, doctors are asked to
indicate if smoking was a cause of death. They
answer yes in a quarter of deaths. Nationally, that
would work out to 531,000 deaths a year.

What can parents and other concerned citizens
do to fight this plague? Here are several suggestions:

Become informed. Subscribe to *Tobacco Youth Reporter*.
Write STAT (Stop Teenage Addiction to Tobacco), 121
Lyman Street 210, Springfield, MA 01103. Get your

kids and/or school involved in The Smokefree America Ad Contest described in Answer 15.

Ban cigarette ads (Answer 16). Congressman Mike Synar (D-Oklahoma) is proposing a bill that would do this. When Norway banned cigarette ads, sales dropped 20 percent.

Prohibit cigarette sales to minors (Answer 16). A citizen group in Allentown, Pennsylvania, sent minors to see if they could buy cigarettes in a state that prohibits sales to those under age sixteen. Most of the stores they went to sold to them. This discovery eventually led to a city law prohibiting cigarette vending machines. A 1992 sting found that only 30 percent of stores continued to sell to minors. STAT has organized similar stings in four cities. To learn more, write them at the above address.

In 1992 Congressman Synar passed a bill that requires states to outlaw sale of tobacco to those under age eighteen or face the loss of up to 40 percent of federal substance abuse funds. With that new muscle in the fight, why not organize your own sting? Send neighborhood kids into local stores. Involve your local newspaper and TV in the project. Hold a kids' press conference. Find out if your community is really law abiding!

Alcohol

Junior and senior high school students consume 1.1 *billion* cans of beer a year. The average youngster's first drinking experience is at age twelve. And why not? By age eighteen a typical kid will have seen seventy-five thousand scenes of alcohol consumption on TV, and drinking is always portrayed as fun. Result: 8 million students in grades seven through twelve drink *weekly.* What's more, almost one-third of high school seniors say it is easy to obtain alcohol or marijuana *at their school.* In the eighth grade, 13 percent of kids do "binge drinking," having five or more drinks in a row within a two week period. By their senior year, 30 percent do so.

The biggest price of teen drinking has been paid on the highways. Before 1970 most states required purchasers of alcohol to be twenty-one. But after the voting age was lowered to eighteen, many states also lowered the drinking age. This resulted in more than a decade of increased alcohol-related deaths for those aged sixteen to twenty. In 1984 Congress required states to return the drinking age to twenty-one if they wanted to receive federal highway aid. Highway deaths of those under age twenty-one fell from 8,315 to 5,749 by 1991!

The Justice Department points to many other problems involving drinking by young people. A third of youth who commit serious crimes consume alcohol just before the offense. More than 70 percent of teenage suicides involve frequent use of alcohol or drugs. And alcohol is a major factor in more than half the rapes reported among college students. What can be done?

Pass "Not a Drop" laws (Answer 17). In Oregon,
the driver's license of any teenage driver found with
any alcohol in his or her blood will be suspended for
ninety days. North Carolina, the first state with a
"Not a Drop" law, goes further: if any alcohol is
found in the blood of a sixteen or seventeen year
old, the young person's license will be confiscated.
Thanks to this law, North Carolina has seen a 60
percent decrease in teen drivers involved in alcohol-
related crashes. Utah recently passed such a law.
What about your state?

Ban ads. In 1992, at a conference in Knoxville
sponsored by the local media and RID (Remove
Intoxicated Drivers) Dr. Koop urged that alcohol
advertising be banned on TV:

> The time has come for the American people
> to protect their children—and themselves—
> from the threat to their health in the guise
> of advertising. . . . Most alcohol advertising
> lies. It associates with romance, glamour, ath-
> letics and worldly success, substances which
> instead lead to disability and death. First
> Amendment protection is not extended to
> speech encouraging illegal activity. Alcohol
> advertisers depend on reaching young
> people. . . . The airwaves belong to the public.
> The public has a right to make sure that the
> airwaves are not exploited for public harm,
> and a ban on alcohol advertising is a compel-
> ling public health concern.

Conduct "stings." Insurance Institute Vice President Charles Hurley urges local towns to conduct "sting" operations to identify and punish stores selling alcohol to youth. In Denver, police cadets younger than twenty-one went into eighty-eight stores in June 1991 and were able to buy six-packs of beer in fifty-two of them. Every store was issued a letter warning they would be prosecuted if it happened again. The cadets returned a year later and only thirty-two of the stores sold alcohol to them. Fourteen merchants were guilty both times: they received license suspensions. Answer 18 tells the results in Albany, New York, where such stings also have been organized.

Raise taxes. One long-range solution is being considered even as I write: Dramatically hike the federal tax on beer, wine, and liquor as well as on cigarettes.

The federal tax on cigarettes (in early 1993) is only twenty-four cents a pack. In Canada the federal tax jumped from forty-six cents in 1980 to $3.27 in 1991. Consumption fell 40 percent, while tax revenue jumped from $1 billion to $7 billion. A similar tax hike in the United States would have three positive effects:

- Smoking by teenagers might drop by *two-thirds*. That's what happened in Canada. In 1979 half of those aged fifteen to ninteen were smokers. Now only 16 percent of teens are smokers! They are less able to pay the six to seven dollar cost of each pack. Overall consumption by Americans would drop by at least a third if the tax rose by three dollars. If the added tax were two dollars, the general public would reduce its consumption by 23 percent according to the Coalition on Smoking OR Health.

- A two dollar tax would, over time, also prevent 1.9 million premature deaths due to smoking, since there would be 7.6 million fewer smokers, according to the Coalition. This is based on the estimate that 434,000 of the nation's 2.2 million deaths per year are due to smoking. In extending nearly two million lives, more years of life would be gained than were lost in all of America's wars combined.

- A two dollar tax would still raise an additional $30 billion a year; a four dollar tax would yield $50 billion, says the Coalition on Smoking OR Health. That's nearly enough to give health insurance to 35 million Americans who do not now have it!

Alcohol kills about a hundred thousand people a year. Yet the federal tax on beer is only a nickel a can, and on a glass of wine only four cents. One standard serving of beer or wine has the same alcohol content as a shot of 80-proof liquor, on which the tax is twelve cents. Beer is responsible for 80 percent of drunk driving deaths. If it were taxed at the same rate as distilled spirits, the new tax would raise $4.5 million a year. If all forms of alcohol taxes were raised even higher to account for inflation since 1970, there would be $23 billion of new federal revenue a year. And there would be ten thousand fewer deaths per year, since higher taxes mean fewer drinkers and fewer drinks per drinker. Certainly, fewer youths could afford a six-pack of beer if the tax were thirty-three cents a can instead of five cents. A six-pack would cost $1.64 more.

Polls show strong support for higher "sin taxes." Three-fourths favor higher taxes on alcohol and cigarettes, especially now that additional sources of federal revenue are being so desperately sought.

Illicit Drugs

A startling poster is seen in schools and businesses around Phoenix, Arizona: *What the casual drug user will be wearing next season* is the headline. Beneath it is a picture: handcuffs on a white male's wrists. At the bottom are the words: *Do drugs. Do time.* That's the first paragraph of Answer 19, which spotlights a strategy that would certainly get the attention of young people tempted to do drugs.

Most drug-enforcement efforts focus on drug dealers. But when they are arrested, others take their place. Phoenix has shifted its focus to users. Everybody caught does time—typically a day or two, plus fines to cover the cost of prison boarding. New Jersey has a similar law with an additional punishment: all who are convicted lose their driver's license for six months to two years. Some 84 percent of students are aware of this law, and 40 percent have admitted that it convinced them not to use drugs.

But what can be done to help those who do become drug addicts? Answer 20 describes one of the most effective solutions available today. Teen Challenge, a rigorous, year-long, biblically based effort, strives to *convert* participants. The spiritual dimension is missing from almost all other programs, and no other program has a success rate equaling that of Teen Challenge: 60 to 80 percent at its 124 centers, which served 12,500 people in 1991. If your son or daughter is really strung out, there is no better answer than Teen Challenge, and there are *no* fees for services. You will find the address of the U.S. headquarters in Answer 20.

15 A n s w e r
Kids Say Don't Smoke

The ad by Melissa Antonow won a prize for fifth graders. It shows the "Marlboro Man" twenty years later, riding his horse out of green mountains into a cemetery. The horse is healthy, but the hero is a skeleton, passing tombstones called *Lung Cancer, Emphysema,* and *Heart Disease.*

The headline says it all: *Come to Where the Cancer Is.*

Another by Jude Dominique, eleventh grade, crushes a huge cigarette out on the back of a dead man on a street. *Put It Out Before It Puts You Out!*

José Vega, seventh grade, drew a cartoon with the top frame showing a boy buying cigarettes, with a headline, *BUY NOW* . . . Below, the ad says *PAY LATER* with the youngster lying in a hospital bed.

CIGARETTES—HARMLESS UNTIL YOU USE THEM, screams another.

These and other ads were on a wonderful poster, "The Smokefree America Ad Contest," announcing the contest in 1991. Below the six winning ads of 1989 was this: *WARNING: Your Ad Is Dangerous to the Tobacco Companies' Wealth.*

Yeah! Right on!

There is a thousand dollar first place prize and five hundred dollar second place prize for each grade ranging from kindergarten and first grade through twelfth grade. If your child has never competed in this contest, I have two suggestions:

1. Buy a copy in any bookstore of the paperback *Kids Say Don't Smoke* (New York: Workman, 1991) for $5.95. It not only has all the previous years' winners, which will inspire your kids, but has wonderful text that will inform your children of the facts.

A page quotes Anthony Bonamassa of Brooklyn's South Shore High School: "In the fall of 1990, two hundred children from Harlem picketed Philip Morris headquarters in New York City, chanting, 'Thou shalt not kill.'" They called on Philip Morris to:

A. Admit that smoking causes diseases:
   —90 percent of lung cancer victims are smokers
   —90 percent of throat cancer victims are smokers
   —90 percent of emphysema victims are smokers
B. Stop pushing cigarettes on children:
   —No more cigarette logos on candy cigarettes
   —No more cigarette billboards near schools

> —No more cigarette billboards near sporting events
> —No more free cigarettes at youth rock concerts
> —No more advertising cigarettes as 'athletic' or 'sexy'
> —No more paying movies to feature teen heroes smoking
>
> C. Stop selling cigarettes without health warnings in underdeveloped countries.

"Philip Morris officials refused to meet with representatives of the demonstrators, who included a priest, a minister, and a rabbi," concludes the text opposite a previous winner's poster.

2. Write Smokefree Educational Services, 375 South End Avenue, Suite 32F, New York, NY 10280 for their newsletter.

Obviously, schools that conduct a Smokefree contest "win" big, even if no student wins. They harness powerful peer pressure to fight the kid-oriented ad campaigns of the cigarette firms. So they save lives.

The "Kids Say Don't Smoke" campaign was started in 1987 by thirty-year-old Joseph Cherner, a bond trader on Wall Street. He is a rare person—a man who made enough money (selling bonds) that he took a leave of absence to fight smoking.

No one has been more effective in fighting this horror that kills 434,000 Americans every year—more than alcohol, drugs, homicide, suicide, car accidents, fires, and AIDS combined. As the child of two parents who died from smoking, I am grateful for his leadership.

A   n   s   w   e   r **16**

Stop Cigarette Sales to Minors

"Smoking is the chief avoidable cause of death in our society," said Dr. C. Everett Koop, America's former surgeon general in his twentieth report to the nation on smoking. Indeed, it kills 434,000 people a year—over one hundred times more than the four thousand people killed by cocaine and heroin addition, and quadruple the number who die of alcohol-related causes.

Yet the society considers drug-related and alcohol-related deaths more serious. Why? Is not the life of a man or woman who dies of lung cancer or heart disease as valuable as that of a heroin addict? Perhaps it is because smoking seems harmless. One doesn't have to steal to pay for the habit. The decision to smoke is considered personal, a freedom guaranteed by the Constitution.

But cigarette companies are selling more than $1 billion in cigarettes a year *to children*. Last year kids under the age of eighteen bought cigarettes from vending machines 450,000 times a day.

In rural Alaska, the U.S. Center for Disease Control found that 17 percent of five-year-old girls used smokeless tobacco—snuff, usually Copenhagen or Skoal. They had used it for an average of 1.3 years!

"A survey of Arkansas kindergarten children found that 21 percent used smokeless tobacco and

36 percent plan to use it in the future," says a report by Dr. Thomas Radecki in *Psychiatric Mental Health and Behavioral Medicine Update*. In Louisiana, a fifth of eight- to nine-year olds use it—an 800 percent jump in the last five years.

"Boxes of snuff are often available free through youth magazines. Rock concerts and sports events are sometimes sponsored by smokeless tobacco companies where free samples are distributed," said the report. "Tobacco companies often sponsor 'spitting contests' at fairs and festivals with prizes to different categories, including preschoolers."

Not only is smokeless tobacco addictive and a cause of premature death due to mouth cancers, but users are likely to go on to cigarettes.

Radecki urges that smokeless tobacco products be banned. Certainly, the soliciting of tiny children should be outlawed, with heavy fines.

In fact, three-fourths of states have laws that prohibit selling tobacco to minors. Illinois' law goes back to 1899. Many require that a sign be posted that indicates a prohibition of sales to minors.

However, according to former Surgeon General C. Everett Koop, 60 percent of smokers began at the age of thirteen or younger! It is easy for kids to buy them, and ads make it seem attractive.

The American Cancer Society says if students haven't begun smoking in high schools, the chances are good that they never will.

Yet only 47 percent of school districts in a recent survey indicated that they had banned smoking, says a November article in *Listen* magazine. Admittedly, enforcing a "No Smoking" policy is difficult. New York State banned it in May 1987, but students report it is common in bathrooms.

Some school officials say they are more concerned about harder drugs than tobacco. This doesn't make sense. The surgeon general's report says smoking is controlled by "a powerfully addicting drug. . . . An extensive body of research has shown that nicotine is the drug in tobacco that causes addiction," said Koop. "Moreover, the process that determines tobacco addiction is similar to those that determine addiction to drugs such as heroin and cocaine." Tobacco addiction leads to other serious addictions.

Rep. Mike Synar (D-Oklahoma) says, "We have a thousand people a day dying from smoking—more than from alcohol, accidents, and drug overdoses combined. It is the largest single preventative cause of death. We spend $4 billion of federal funds in Medicare and Medicaid, and had $23 billion of extra insurance costs because of smoking-related illnesses."

His target is cigarette advertising which he says is "clearly directed toward children" for a good reason: "The industry loses two million of its most loyal customers each year from death or from people quitting," says Cliff Douglass of the American Lung Association. "They must replace five thousand smokers every day with new customers to break even. The surgeon general found that 80 percent of all smokers started by age twenty. Virtually all new customers come from the ranks of children and teenagers. So ads target those potential new smokers."

"Tobacco firms don't hesitate to give free samples at rock and roll concerts—but not at Frank Sinatra concerts." Synar said. "They claim their ads are to get people to switch brands, but only 10 percent switch with $2 billion in sales. Why spend $2 billion on ads for $2 billion in sales?"

Previously this column put a spotlight on an effort by a group called Doctors Ought to Care (DOC) in Decatur, Illinois, to halt the sales of cigarettes to children. They hired an eleven-year-old and a fourteen-year-old to see if stores would sell to them. Some 78 percent did so. DOC went to the chamber of commerce, the mayor, and school principals and got support for a campaign to help fight child cigarette smoking. But 60 percent of the stores were still selling to minors.

In that column I suggested that DOC had a model that should be used in other communities, and I invited readers to tell me of their results. One who did so was Teri St. John of the Allentown, Pennsylvania, Health Department: "We have conducted quarterly undercover operations using minors who volunteer to buy cigarettes followed by a citation from a police officer. The next day, the *Morning Call* publishes the account to help publicize the fact that these sales are illegal. Unfortunately, we cannot say that the rate of sales has declined as a result of this effort," she said. "Each operation yields the majority of merchants still willing to sell to minors, even when fined by the police. Unmonitored vending machines were targeted in our last effort—with some clerks even providing change for the machine."

I want to commend the *Morning Call*'s initiative. Not only has it made a reporter and photographer available, but it has written strong editorials. "It may not be news in the under sixteen population of Allentown who smoke cigarettes that the coffin nails they puff are freely available to them in many of the city's retail outlets. But this news will be of interest to the proprietors of the following Allentown mercantile establishments," all of whom sold to a fifteen-year-old boy.

It noted that the law had been on the books since 1901, "well before anybody had ever heard of the U.S. surgeon general or his warning."

"It is time for the city of Allentown to cite those merchants who continue to violate the law," it said in 1985.

That has been done. But according to reporter Ann Wlazelek, "Of the last six merchants cited, half were dismissed because they involved vending machines," which merchants said could not be watched at all times.

Therefore, the Health Department urged the city council to pass a law eliminating vending machines in public areas frequented by youngsters. Not only did that not pass, but city council members grumbled about the time the Health Department was spending (a day a quarter) on this matter.

To quote the surgeon general, "With the evidence that tobacco is addicting, is it appropriate for tobacco products to be sold through vending machines, which are easily accessible to children? Should the sale of tobacco be treated less seriously than the sale of alcoholic beverages, for which a specific license is required (and revoked for repeated sales to minors)?"

Reporter Ann Wlazelek courageously adds, "I'm proud to see this newspaper in the forefront of this issue, and I'd like to see it extend to its advertising policy as well." Cigarette ads are a big source of revenue and would really test any publication's commitment to the smoking problem.

Fortunately, there are a number of cities that have enacted a total ban on vending machines to reduce the access of youth to them. In California alone they are banned in Sacramento, San Luis Obispo, and Santa Monica, and they are banned across the country in cities such as Ann Arbor, Michigan; Orono, Maine; and Lenox, Massachusetts.

Why not try to ban vending machines in your community?

17 A n s w e r

Citizens Organize "Not a Drop" Laws

Oregon became the fourth state to enact a "not a drop" law when it comes to teen drunk driving. Any teenage driver found with any alcohol in his or her blood will have a license suspended for ninety days.

The penalty stiffens if the teen refuses the test, is prosecuted, or is a repeat offender. Oregon's law was sparked by many fatal accidents involving drunk teens, according to Joan Plank of the state's Department of Motor Vehicles.

North Carolina, the first to enact such a law, has a simpler standard. Any teen driver with alcohol in the blood loses a license until age eighteen! Its impact has been dramatic: a 60 percent decrease in the incidence of teen drivers involved in alcohol-related crashes, according to John Lacey, the former director of the Highway Safety Research Center at the University of North Carolina. He says that the law has had a big impact on those aged nineteen and over, as well as those eighteen and under.

Maine and Wisconsin have also passed "not a drop" laws. Every other state should consider such a step. Teen drunk drivers were involved in fifteen hundred fatalities in 1989. However, there is also a need for a crackdown on those businesses who sell beer, wine, or liquor to minors. Why should adults who profit from selling minors intoxicating beverages get away with it?

What can be done? Consider what happened in Greensboro, North Carolina, a few years ago. Its police department asked some teenagers to walk into eighty different businesses to see if they could purchase liquor. The teens were told to present valid identification if asked. But in more than two-thirds of the cases, the merchants did not ask for IDs. All were prosecuted. Most received fines. When repeated some months later, the percentage convicted dropped—but was still over 50 percent.

Why couldn't this be done in your own community?

I was invited to speak at an ethics class at Geneva College in Beaver Falls, Pennsylvania. After speaking for a while on ethics, I suggested that the ethics class itself could take on this project: "How many students here are aged nineteen or twenty?" I asked. Most raised their hands. "You could go to the Beaver Falls police and offer to test the willingness of local merchants to sell to minors. This class could have a profound effect on how ethics are practiced in Beaver Falls."

The students remained impassive. Not one said it was a good idea. Perhaps what was running through their minds was the possibility they would be considered traitors to friends who drink. Courage is rare these days. But any police force could find young people willing to be decoys. Some young police officers under age twenty-one would be perfect prospects.

Why isn't this tactic being used more widely? There are several possibilities—none of which reflect well on the commitment to enforcing law on the part of most American communities:

1. Teen drunk driving is not considered a problem even though it is the major cause of death of American teenagers.
2. Many police are alcohol abusers and do not think the issue important.
3. There have been no demands by citizens to enforce the law.

I suspect the problem in most cities is the latter.

The police have never been urged by taxpayers to put a spotlight on those merchants who make money off illegal sales to minors. If that is the case, you contribute to the problem. And *you* could be part of the solution. Let me offer what I hope will be an incentive. Any citizen or law enforcement officer who organizes a "teen drinking decoy" program should write me in care of this publishing house—and tell me of your results.

I will put a spotlight on your work to encourage other good citizens.

A   n   s   w   e   r **18**

"Stings" Reduce Alcohol Sales to Minors

"It's becoming easy for underage people to buy alcohol," said Brian O'Neill, president of the Insurance Institute for Highway Safety (IIHS), based on experiments it conducted of having nineteen- and twenty-year-olds attempt to buy beer in New York state and Washington, D.C.

In Washington, ninety-seven stores out of one hundred sold beer to three minors without asking for identification to prove they were twenty-one. In Westchester County, New York, eighty-two retail outlets out of one hundred and three approached did so. But in the Albany/Schenectady area, only forty-four out of one hundred convenience and liquor stores sold to minors—the same youths involved in the Washington and Westchester IIHS experiments.

Why the sharp difference? "Albany is the only place where they are doing something to enforce the law," said Dr. David Preusser, president of PRG, Inc. in Bridgeport, Connecticut, which conducted the study for IIHS.

But in most cases the law is not enforced. IDs are rarely asked for by store clerks—even in liquor stores—who could lose their license by selling to minors.

(The publicity of the IIHS sting in Washington did prompt D.C. police to use decoys and to charge twenty-two stores with selling to minors. But they were simply fined five hundred dollars. That's so little that a liquor store could sell booze to minors for only a day to pay the fine.)

Beer is the drug of choice on college campuses—despite the recent drug bust at three fraternities at the University of Virginia. UVA's associate dean of students, Sybil Todd, told the *Washington Post* that alcohol was involved "in every instance" of date rape on campus.

"There's almost no relationship between other drugs (besides alcohol) and unwanted sex or property damage," said another UVA official. At Towson State in Baltimore County, 98 percent of cases where students were charged with conduct violations, alcohol—not drugs—was an involving factor.

"What's especially disturbing," said IIHS's O'Neill, "is that while underage people are buying alcohol with ease, the proportion of fatally injured drivers in this age group with high blood alcohol concentration is on the rise after years of decline."

In 1980, 53 percent of all drivers under age

twenty-one who died in crashes had blood alcohol concentration (BAC) of 0.1 or higher. By 1987, after most states raised the legal age to twenty-one for buying alcohol, only 28 percent of underage youth dying in accidents had illegal BAC levels. But by 1989 the percent was up to 32 percent. Only youths showed that increase, says IIHS.

Despite all efforts to get drunk drivers off the road, the odds against police catching an alcohol-impaired driver are a thousand to one, said James Kolstad, chairman of the National Transportation Safety Board.

Therefore, it is essential that local police be nudged to enforce the law. My suggestion is that PTAs or other citizen groups use underage decoys to test local retailers. The IIHS embarrassed Washington to act.

Albany police chief John Dale said his department "has been making a concerted effort with a sting team" for years, "aggressively enforcing state liquor laws, arresting clerks, owners, and bartenders. We have had numerous [license] suspensions."

No wonder most Albany stores did not sell to the IIHS-planted minors. You could organize a similar effort with some committed students acting as decoys.

A   n   s   w   e   r *19*

Tough Laws Reduce Drug Demand

A startling poster is seen in schools and businesses around Phoenix, Arizona: *What the casual drug user will be wearing next season* is the headline. Beneath it is a picture: handcuffs on a white male's wrists. At the bottom are the words: *Do drugs. Do time.*

The fine print explains it all in one paragraph: "A tough new anti-drug police task force is now on the streets in Maricopa County [Arizona] enforcing our already tough drug laws. And if they catch you with drugs, they're taking you to jail. You then face felony charges; a prison sentence and stiff financial penalties. Or pay to enter a year-long rehab program. All of which means drugs are no longer the fashionable thing to do."

This is a radically new strategy. Most police departments look the other way when they find a casual user of drugs. He or she is seen as the victim. The villain is the drug dealer against whom 90 percent of police resources are directed. He is the one who makes the big money and is behind the soaring killings of many cities. But in Maricopa County, former Sheriff Tom Agnos says: "We have elevated the user to the same level as the drug dealer and trafficker. The user is not a victim, but is every bit as guilty of the evil of illicit drug use."

At a conference sponsored by The Heritage Foundation, he said, "For twenty-five years we have been going after the dealer, but the traffic side of the problem did not go away. Are we attacking the right part of the problem on the supply side? We have had no success whatsoever. So we began to look at the user. In sum, we can have an impact if the drug user does time. Enforcement gets publicity. It educates. And it provides an opportunity for rehabilitation."

Some twenty-one different law enforcement agencies in and around Phoenix decided to share resources to go after the casual drug user. "We have zero tolerance. Everybody goes to jail no matter what amount of drug was involved. It may be for an hour up to a couple of days," said Agnos.

If the drug user has had no previous convictions in the last year, he is eligible for a diversion program offering treatment. There are opportunities for rehabilitation, but he must pay his way ranging from one thousand dollars for marijuana to three thousand dollars for cocaine for treatment for up to a year, with frequent urine checks.

"And he must pay fifty dollars a day for every day in jail—like staying in Holiday Inn!" he said with a twinkle. In the first year, there were five thousand arrests, half of whom were diverted for treatment costing them four hundred thousand dollars.

New Jersey launched a similar program in 1987 that arrested sixty-five thousand casual drug users in 1989. With overcrowded county jails, the punishment is different—but is "cheap and hurtful," said Ron Susswein, assistant to New Jersey's attorney general. "They get people's attention and don't cost a whole lot. A cash penalty is mandatory. It ranges from a minimum of five hundred to three thousand dollars. The amount is fixed, depending on the drug. If you can't pay immediately, a payment schedule is set up." In 1990, $11 million collected in the program Drug Enforcement Demand Reduction (DEDR) was returned to local communities for treatment and enforcement.

A second level of punishment for all who are convicted is an automatic loss of a driver's license for at least six months and possibly up to two years. If a person is under the state's minimum driving age of seventeen, the penalty is imposed when one reaches age seventeen! Susswein says, "What we are trying to do is provide one additional reason or excuse for people to 'say no to drugs.' The dominant theory behind punishment is that it hurts." And that makes it a deterrent.

When he goes to high schools and explains DEDR, hands shoot up and kids say, "This is unconstitutional!" Nonsense. The right to drive is a privilege, given or taken by the state. Parents understand and applaud. So far, about twenty-five thousand lost their driver's license for drug possession.

Is this approach of punishing casual drug users having an effect? A survey of New Jersey students found only 16 percent did not know about the law. Some 40 percent said the law strongly influenced their decision not to use drugs. As one kid put it, "I won't risk my license for that crap." But 25 percent said the law made no difference—mostly inner city kids who have no license or car.

In Maricopa County, Arizona, there is even more important evidence that punishment works. In 1988, more than 50 percent of those arrested for any crime had been using drugs. In 1989, that dropped to 45 percent. Phoenix now has a lower percentage of those arrested who test positive for drug use than almost any other major metropolitan area.

There is a way to reduce the demand for drugs in America.

A n s w e r **20**

"Teen Challenge" Helps Addicts Change

Several years ago I came upon a program to help runaway youth in Brooklyn called Teen Challenge. It wasn't working with the big numbers other shelters were, but it had an 86 percent success rate of those who completed a rigorous yearlong, biblically based effort.

The Teen Challenge model is now in 110 cities, helping several thousand addicts find new life. As Rev. Jim Allen told a Teen Challenge center in District Heights, Maryland, "John 1:12 says God 'gave us power to become sons of God.'" Several replied, "Amen!"

"The problem with secular programs is that they call addiction sickness. It is a sin problem," said Aaron, twenty-one, an addict who once sold up to five thousand dollars a day of crack. "Drugs is only part of your whole problem. Secular programs don't focus on sin, that you need Jesus Christ in your life. That is the only answer to the sin problem."

"I came here to find salvation through Jesus Christ," said Willy, thirty-six. "I was doing things I knew I could get away with: drugs, robbery, adultery, fornication, whatever you can think of. And I had two businesses: home renovations and modifying computers. I was over my head. In Teen Challenge . . . I'm getting closer to God and regaining self-control. I can do the right thing without someone standing over me."

Half of these men were white. Only one is a teen-ager, Chris, seventeen. Just a month ago he was in a juvenile prison where a man from a church came to speak. Out of boredom, Chris went to hear him. To his surprise, he made a commitment to Christ. The chaplain gave him a copy of *The Cross and the Switchblade,* a best-seller about how Dave Wilker-son began Teen Challenge.

"I wanted to go to Teen Challenge, but with my fifteen charges, I thought I'd get twenty years. I went to court and all charges were dropped! It was a miracle. I came to Teen Challenge the next day. I came on my own. I could have gone home, but I told my mom I need to get spiritual help. I am happy and secure here. God's helping me through everything. I can succeed."

Bob, forty-two, was not so lucky. "I've been a her-oin addict twenty-three years. I was a clinical psy-chologist and off drugs seven years. My marriage broke up. I got into heroin, ending up with a huge $250-a-day habit. I sold heroin, did a tour of local jails and two years in prison. I lost everything," he said.

"I'm now traveling in the Holy Spirit. I have a power I could never depend on before. I believe I will receive answers. I'm completely at peace here, unlike what I've found in secular rehabilitation. I feel I've come home. What's happened is a miracle. This place is anointed by God."

Catherine Hess, a creator of a program in New

York that gives methadone to heroin addicts, was skeptical until she saw addicts five years after graduating from Brooklyn's Teen Challenge. Interviews and urine tests revealed 86 percent were clean! She called Teen Challenge "unique and successful." Other Teen Challenge centers have 60 to 70 percent success.

To learn more, write Teen Challenge, Box 9871M, Springfield, MO 65801.

Teach Christian Values

In 1990 the Girl Scouts released a disturbing study conducted by pollster Louis Harris of five thousand elementary, junior- and senior-high students in public, private, and parochial schools. It was designed to examine the "moral compasses" of America's children. When the results came in, nearly half (45 percent) said their moral compass was their "own personal experience." A scant 16 percent stated they made moral choices based on "what God or Scripture tells [them] is right."

Yet 82 percent of those polled say, "There is a God." Gallup polls confirm that seven of ten teenagers say they are "religious persons." And 90 percent pray. So what accounts for situational ethics reigning supreme among teens? Sadly, we have to look no further than the moral laxity of their parents! Gallup reported in 1992 that 69 percent of Americans agree with this statement and only 27 percent disagree: "There are few moral absolutes: what is right or wrong usually varies from situation to situation."

You would not be reading this book unless you were among the quarter of Americans who believe there *are* moral absolutes. The question is, how can those values best be taught to the young—especially to our own kids in a culture that honors Madonna more than Mary, Prince more than the Prince of Peace? (Only 15 of 2,037 secondary students recently surveyed said religious people are their heros; 1,065 named actors/actresses; 529, musicians; 312, athletes.)

One encouraging finding: 64 percent of youngsters turn to their parents for advice when they "don't know what the right thing is to do." But that declines with age. In high school 58 percent go to peers first.

Thus it is essential for parents to actively teach biblical values to give kids powerful rudders to guide them away from evil and toward purity and integrity. But how can this best be done? This chapter explores four practical strategies parents can use to introduce Judeo-Christian values so that they become the guiding principles of your children's lives:

Character education programs (Answers 21, 22, and 23). Public schools can teach such principles as honesty, courage, and selflessness. They can do this without using Scripture, and they can gain the support of even secular parents (quite a trick!). The Jefferson Center for Character Education has had astounding success—unfortunately, its program is not well known, and bureaucrats in some school districts resist using their materials.

Former president Bush and fifty governors

agreed on six national educational goals, some of which are unlikely ever to be achieved without character education. For example, one goal is that schools be "free of violence and drugs and offer a disciplined environment conducive to learning." How is it possible for students to become the "first in the world in mathematics and science achievement" unless they develop the heart, will, drive, and discipline needed to succeed? Can character education do that? Answer 23 shows that a year after character education was piloted in thirty-one Los Angeles schools, major disciplinary problems (weapons, drugs, and fighting) had fallen 25 percent and minor disciplinary problems had plunged 39 percent.

If character education can work in the inner city, the odds are in favor of successfully teaching strong values and good behavior to almost any student. Read how several school districts have benefited, and learn how you can get materials for your own children to use.

Camping programs (Answer 24). Another way to influence kids' values can be through a solid summer camping program. Most camps offer opportunities to swim or canoe. But a few go beyond sports to character development. Answer 24 describes such a camp that my boys were fortunate enough to attend. Like many camps established early in the twentieth century, Camp Agawam in Raymond, Maine, makes powerful use of the "Woodcraft Laws" drafted by an early promoter of the Boy Scouts, Ernest Thompson Seton. These laws, built around the four themes of beauty, truth, fortitude, and love, are restated around the campfire in ceremonies boys love. Not every child can go to summer camp, but every parent can use the Woodcraft principles. Why not adapt them to your own home?

Church youth groups (Answer 25). Parents, don't just dump your kids in the nearest Sunday school. Search out the best Sunday school and youth program in your area, and enroll them there. A strong church youth program is a parent's most important ally in Christianizing one's children, especially when they enter junior high and hormones begin to rage.

A well-run program will attract flocks of teens not just on Sunday mornings, but at retreats, in athletic leagues, and even in evangelistic outreach to other youth. Parents, read Answer 25 to learn about the possibilities. Church youth directors, read it to see how your own programs measure up.

Parental teaching (Answer 26). We parents can't leave all the moral teaching to others. We must personally teach our children the truths of Scripture on a regular basis. I have to confess that I did not do a good job in this area. At times I'd read some Scripture at the dinner table, but it was not well received. However, before Christmas, 1992, I learned of several very creative Christmas gifts, including a unique gift created by a father in

Texas. It is a special placemat covered with hundreds of biblical references, which he calls "Daily Guidelines to Strong and Happy Christian Families." Parents can use these placemats to help families learn and discuss key biblical principles at the dinner table, and so weave them into family life.

A n s w e r **21**

Character Education
Gives Kids a Moral Anchor

"Train a child in the way he should go, and when he is old he will not turn from it," says Proverbs 22:6. That's why 90 percent of parents want their children to get religious instruction, says the Gallup poll. One result: 86 percent of those aged eighteen to twenty-four believe in the divinity of Christ. But some 47 percent of school students say they'd cheat on an exam. America's parents and churches are doing a poor job teaching ethics. That grim conclusion is inescapable in reading the landmark *Girl Scouts Survey on the Beliefs and Moral Values of America's children.*

When pollster Louis Harris questioned five thousand children in elementary, junior, and senior high schools, he found only 16 percent said they made moral judgments based on "what God or Scripture tells [them] is right."

A fifth say they take an adult's advice, but that number drops as kids get older. (By high school, kids turn to peers for advice.) Nearly half (45 percent) said their moral compass was their "own personal experience." Didn't their churches teach

Proverbs 16:2: "All a man's ways seem innocent to him." Apparently not. The result: poor moral choices.

Students were asked, "If you were unsure of what was right or wrong in a situation, how would you decide what to do?" Some 18 percent said they'd do "what makes me happy"; 10 percent would do "what would get me ahead." Such students are three times as likely to cheat on an exam or have premarital sex as those who "do what Scripture says."

Professor James Hunter, a sociologist at the University of Virginia who wrote the report, says, "These kids are in different moral solar systems. Depending on the moral assumptions they live by, they will approach a moral dilemma in fundamentally different ways. The influence of these moral assumptions is more important than social class, race, or gender." That is a finding that will shock most sociologists who assume that "environment has the greatest impact."

For example, 44 percent of kids whose families earn more than forty thousand dollars would cheat on an exam versus 39 percent of those with incomes below twenty thousand dollars. Surprisingly, more affluent children are more morally confused! In any case, the difference is small compared to the three to one differential noted above.

The students were asked how they'd make practical ethical choices:

"You have had a steady relationship for a long time and you feel very much in love. At this point your girlfriend or boyfriend tells you she or he wants to have sex with you. In this situation, would you 1) have sex; 2) try to hold off if you can; 3) refuse to have sex for now; 4) insist on waiting for marriage." Some 37 percent of junior and senior high kids would have sex; 38 percent would hold off; and 24 percent would wait for marriage. But 54 percent who believe in doing what feels good would have sex, while only 19 percent of those who follow Scripture would do so.

"You go to a party where some of your friends are drinking alcohol. Someone hands you a drink." In this situation, only 52 percent of junior high students and 40 percent of high schoolers would refuse the drink. But 79 percent of those with a Judeo-Christian perspective would say no versus 33 percent of those who do what feels good or what might get them ahead.

In between the extremes on a moral compass are those who take a "civic humanist" point of view and do "what is best for everyone." But that vague moral view comes closer to an expressivist "doing what feels good."

"Some school property has been destroyed. Your best friend brags to you that he did it. The school principal asks if you know what happened." On this issue, 50 percent of the expressivists and 43 percent of civic humanists would deny knowledge of vandalism, versus only 19 percent of the theists.

What about the role of parents? They can have impact. Some 44 percent of students whose parents rarely discipline would lie to the principal compared to 33 percent of students whose parents usually discipline.

The study concludes: "It is not enough to 'just say no' to drugs or any other undesirable behavior. Children are capable of moral reasoning and adults would do well to cultivate this." Hunter added in an interview: "We need to recognize that children are not moral slot machines. They are not only capable of understanding reasons, but they need reasons."

Fortunately, it is possible to teach ethics. Character education can even be taught in public schools. One year after the Jefferson Center for Character Education introduced a curriculum to the Robert Lewis Stevenson Intermediate School in Honolulu, daily attendance rose; out-of-school suspensions dropped from 12 percent to 7 percent; in-school suspensions fell from 36 to 19 percent. And those on the honor roll rose from 26 to 36 percent.

What can be taught? Honesty, courage, punctuality, sexual abstinence, perseverance, etc. To learn more, write Jefferson Center for Character Education, 202 S. Lake Ave., Pasadena, CA 91101.

22 *A n s w e r*
Character Classes Help to Meet National Education Goals

"Schools across America have simply refused to take responsibility for the character of their students," says Kathleen Kennedy Townsend, who runs a program to spark Maryland kids to try community service. "They wash their hands of the teaching of virtue, doing little to create an environment that teaches children the importance of self-discipline, obligation, and civic participation. As one teacher training text says, 'There is no right or wrong answer to any question of value.'"

Of all children under the age of twenty who died in 1987, a tenth died of gunshot wounds, and gunshot injuries of kids aged sixteen and under soared 300 percent since 1966.

But there is hope. In Baltimore, the number of incidents on school property involving guns plunged from 122 in 1983–84 to 35 in 1989, and other serious incidents, such as assaults, robberies, and rapes, fell by half.

One reason is that Baltimore appointed a Character and Citizenship Commission, which decided that honesty, respect for others, discipline, courage, citizenship, patriotism and a sense of justice could be taught.

As a result of reading my column on character education, they turned to the Jefferson Center for Character Education that developed character education materials used in Baltimore. Only a few goals needed fresh curricular materials in addition to those from the Jefferson Center for Character Education. Teachers agreed to set aside twenty minutes a day in each elementary school to teach the material, and they were trained in 1984–85. "We did nothing before the 1985–86 school year, and checked a month and a half later and found 95 percent of the teachers had picked up the materials on their own and begun teaching," said James

Sarnecki, coordinator of adult and alternative education.

"Our approach in the past was negative," said Edna Greer, principal of Mount Washington Elementary School. "'Don't do this. Don't do that.' Now our approach is positive."

On Wednesday morning, kindergarten tykes speaking in unison over a loudspeaker said, "Our word for today is *Caring.*" Other days the focus may be on Common Sense, Cooperation, Consideration, or Courtesy: "The five Cs."

Moments later, a first-grade teacher in her classroom said, "I have a box of crayons. I know I should not have them out. I am doing exactly what I want to do. Is that person a caring person?"

"No!" they replied.

"How does he show he cares?"

"By listening," said a boy. "By giving respect," chimed another.

Upstairs in the fifth grade, Michael McNally was more sophisticated. "I want you to tell me some problems on the playground or in the cafeteria." As the children replied, he wrote their comments on the blackboard: "People running in cafeteria without permission. Not following directions. Fighting. When kids are hurt, no one comes."

Then he said, "Will you try to come up with solutions? Let's do some brainstorming. Break up in small groups, for each of the five Cs. We'll have five group leaders. I'll give you five minutes to see what you can come up with." He handed each leader a heart with one of the *C* words (*caring, cooperation,* etc.) written on it.

At the Cooperation table a girl said, "Talking it out rather than fighting." Another added, "Cooperating when you don't want to." One boy said, "When you get on someone's nerves, you should leave."

What's the program's impact? "Before we had character education, ten children a week were sent to me for discipline," said Greer. "Now I have only one a week." Thus, students can develop a conscience and a knowledge of how to solve interpersonal problems. But sadly, Mount Washington is not using all of the character education materials, and some Baltimore schools use none.

The Abell Foundation offered to pay for a coordinator but bureaucrats stalled. "We don't understand it," said Abell President Bob Embry. "Parents are enthusiastic about it. School officials don't give it importance."

The Jefferson materials cost *only two dollars per student,* including monthly posters on such themes as honesty, and curriculum materials to teach "Twelve Responsibility Skills: Steps to Success." Like what? "Be a doer. Be a listener. Be confident. Be a goal-setter. Be a risk-taker."

Jefferson's president David Brooks says, "We are trying to teach the basic language and concepts of particular values that can be translated into behavior. We think kids have these ideas. They don't."

One lesson on being a goal-setter has the teacher ask, "What is a goal? How does goal-setting affect me or my school?" Many kids can't visualize this afternoon, let alone next month. Another lesson asks, "How does being a goal-setter affect the community?" This widens the focus.

The posters ask, "How can I show courage? How can I be honest?"

The values are all Judeo-Christian, but stated in nonreligious terms acceptable in public schools. Ten minutes a day of talk on these values could change America.

Former President George Bush and the nation's governors agreed to "National Educational Goals." Bush said, "I want to see these goals posted on the wall in every school, so that all who walk in—the parents, students, teachers—know what we're aiming for."

The goals for the year 2000 are so important that I've listed them here. But as you look them over, do you see something that is missing?

1. All children in America will start school ready to learn.
2. The high school graduate rate will increase to at least 90 percent.
3. U.S. students will leave grades four, eight, and twelve having demonstrated competency over challenging subject matter, including English, mathematics, science, history, and geography, and every school will ensure that all students are prepared for citizenship, further learning, and productive employment.
4. U.S. students will be the first in the world in mathematics and science achievement.

5. Every adult American will be literate and will possess the skills necessary to compete in a global economy.

6. Every school will be free of violence and drugs and offer a disciplined environment conducive to learning.

What's missing is a clear strategy for achieving the toughest of these goals—providing the motivation to students now lacking it, to become disciplined, well-educated, and committed enough as students to graduate from high school and be ready for college or to work in a global economy. There is a way to give students the heart, will, and drive needed to succeed. It is called "character education."

"A school is an island where adults control the language," says Dr. David Brooks, president of the Jefferson Center for Character Education, which developed a character ed curriculum. "We alter the thinking to focus on what we want kids to do, rather than on what we don't want them to do. We are in the same business as Ford. We are advertising socially responsible behavior."

Teachers are given discussion materials with four lessons for each of the twelve skills. The first lesson asks kids to define terms. "Be here," for example, means being physically and mentally present, ready for work. A teacher might say, "Be friendly means when you hear a racial slur, you don't talk like that. A risk-taker will tell the offender to stop it."

Or she might ask, "How does being a goal-setter affect you personally or the community?" Initially, she will get blank stares. Kids are very present-oriented and have difficulty thinking in long-range terms. This is especially true in politics. Kids don't understand plans, strategy, etc.

Each month a different poster asks a Question Of The Month: "How can I be honest?" "How can I show courage?" "How can I keep my commitments?"

There are forty-five thousand classrooms now using the materials. Tennessee now requires character education in all schools. New Hampshire is gearing up.

Unless character education is added to American public schools, we might as well abandon those goals of schools free of violence and drugs, of schools being first in the world in math, or of slashing dropouts. To learn more, write the Jefferson Center for Character Education (see Answer 21 for an address).

23 *A n s w e r*

School Program Teaches Ethics

During the Los Angeles riots, a horrified bystander said, "These people are bringing their kids into stores to loot the stores with them!"

Who is going to teach these kids values? Certainly not the parents. Political liberals and conservatives who hammered out a so-called "Communitarian Platform" have an answer: "We strongly urge that all educational institutions (from kindergartens to universities) recognize and take seriously the grave responsibility to provide moral education. Suggestions that schools participate actively in moral education are often opposed."

Indeed, when Los Angeles was considering "values education" as a possible way to reduce juvenile crime, L.A. County supervisor Gloria Molina asked, "Which values?"

"Our response is straightforward," says the Communitarian Platform. "We ought to teach those values Americans share, for example, that the dignity of all persons ought to be respected, that tolerance is a virtue and discrimination abhorrent, that peaceful resolution of conflicts is superior to violence, that generally truth-telling is morally superior to lying, that democratic government is morally superior to totalitarianism and authoritarianism, that one ought to give a day's work for a day's pay, that saving for one's own . . . future is better than squandering one's income and relying on others to attend to one's future needs."

Committees of the Synagogue Council of America and of the National Conference of Catholic Bishops issued a similar joint report in May 1992, saying parents need all the help they can get from schools in teaching values.

Children are not born with values any more than they are born with math and reading skills. But can values be taught? Absolutely. The non-profit Jefferson Center for Character Education has developed a superb curriculum that has been taught in forty-five thousand classrooms. It is called "How to Be Successful in Less than Ten

Minutes a Day." "It contains 180 daily lessons that teach, in a systematic manner, the concepts of personal responsibility and its relationship to successful behavior," says a teachers' guide. "All truly successful human beings" have "sound ethical principles and a strong self-concept. . . . Since we are not successful in isolation, but are successful only in our contribution to others, a sound code of ethics is essential for the success of individuals and society."

Each month, a different theme is introduced with posters, with bold themes: "How Can I Be of Service to Others?" "Success through Accepting Responsibility," "How Can I Make Good Choices?" "How Can I Show Courage?"

Among "Twelve Steps to Success" are "Be Confident. Be on Time. Be Friendly. Be Prepared. Be a Listener. Be a Doer. Be a Risk-Taker."

For example, to teach risk-taking, the teacher may say, "Successful people have courage and are willing to run the risk of failure. They know that eventually they will reach their goals if they keep trying." An example: "The Wright brothers tested more than two hundred wing models in a wind tunnel before they were able to design a glider that could fly. Don't you imagine they risked embarrassment?" The next day, students are asked to complete sentences: "The risk you take when you study for a test instead of socializing with friends is . . ." They are asked what these thoughts mean: "Dream the impossible dream; reach for the stars; every time you try, you risk success; dare to say no."

The Values Education was piloted in thirty-one
Los Angeles schools in 1990–91, and its impact was
measured by Californian Survey Research. The
results were dramatic. Major disciplinary problems
(weapons, drugs, fighting) fell 25 percent in an average month. Minor disciplinary problems requiring
the intervention of a principal plunged 39 percent.
Suspensions dropped by 16 percent, tardiness by 40
percent, and unexcused absences by 18 percent!
And 92 percent of administrators wanted teachers to
spend more time teaching values. Why? They saw
"students acting more responsibly, did not blame
others, and resisted peer pressure and generally
understood concepts of respect, honesty, and
responsibility more" in spring 1991 than in 1990.

If the material is so great, what about the L.A.
riots? "I can't prove we will make kids perfectly
good," said Jefferson's director Pat McCarthy. "All
we do is show that we can have better odds. It is
no different from parents. They can't guarantee
their children will be wonderful adults."

A n s w e r *24*

Camp Program Models Ethics Training

It was the final "Council Fire" of Camp Agawam, a
lovely spot in the Sebago Lake region of Maine.
The camp's four "tribes"—each wearing a different
feather—marched in and sat in a circle around the
huge bonfire. Seated beneath the totem pole in full
Indian headdress was "Sachem" Dave Mason, sixty-
five, the camp's owner and son of its founder.

Following a ritual developed in the 1920s by

Ernest Thompson Seton, a founder of the Wood-craft League of America, Sachem asked for "sand paintings" to be made around the fire. Using lightly colored sand, four geometric designs were made on the ground around the campfire. A small black pot was put in the center of each.

Then each tribal chief, who had been elected by his tribe's boys, came forward and lit a fire in the small pot as he said three of the 12 "Woodcraft Laws." All of this seemed simply quaint or charming until I heard those "laws" which have little to do with wood—and much to do with basic Judeo-Christian values.

The Woodcraft Laws are stated positively around four themes: beauty, truth, fortitude, and love, the complete text of which follows:

Beauty: Be clean, both yourself and the place you live in.

Understand and respect your body, for it is the temple of the spirit.

Be a friend to all harmless wildlife. Conserve the woods and flowers and especially be ready to fight wild fire in forest and town.

Truth: Word of honor is sacred.

Play fair; foul play is treachery.

Be reverent; worship the Great Spirit and respect all worship of him by others.

Fortitude: Be brave. Courage is the noblest of all attainments.

Be silent while your elders are speaking or otherwise show them deference.

Obey. Obedience is the first duty of the
woodcrafter.
Love: Be kind; do at least one act of unbargain-
ing service each day.
Be helpful; do your share of the work.
Be joyful; seek the joy of being alive.

Is there anyone who could not agree with the
importance of teaching young people these ethical
principles? At Agawam, the boys not only knew
them, but practiced them, inspired by Dave Mason
and his thirty staffers, most of whom are college
students.

At one point in each Council Fire, counselors
stand up and praise those "braves" who have "performed an act of service above and beyond the call
of duty, or who have shown exceptional sportsmanship during the previous week."

How wonderful, I thought, saddened by how
unusual it is to see young people given public
praise for acts of love, rather than acts of competition. Our schools say sportsmanship is important,
but the laurels go to high scorers regardless of how
the points were won. Children hear "Love thy
neighbor" in church, yet they are often encouraged by parents to discriminate against others who
are socially, racially, or religiously different. And so
much attention is placed on high academic
achievement that many students rationalize their
cheating as an acceptable means to attain that goal
rather than achieving good grades through hard
work.

Many of the walking wounded respond by lashing out at the world. One boy at Agawam, for example, came from a high-achieving but broken home. Lacking self-respect and hostile toward others, he was always in fights or throwing temper tantrums. For a while it looked is if he would have to be sent home because he was so disruptive.

But another aspect of Agawam saved the boy, whom we'll call Tom. Each week the counselors privately assigned a personality goal to every camper, called "Katiaki." That's an Indian word meaning "among the chosen few," because those who earned the Katiaki on a given week are publicly identified at the Council Fire and given a candle to lead the boys back to their cabins. "What we are looking for in Katiakis is effort, not perfection," Dave Mason would say. So when Tom complained that he wasn't good enough to play soccer or go sailing, his counselor assigned him Katiakis to try. That was something he could do and for which he'd get a campwide recognition. Tom would then whine, "I don't have any friends." One counselor responded, "The Golden Rule is to love others as you love yourself. But you don't love yourself, so you can't love others. You are special." Through Katiakis, Tom began to love himself and others.

A number of the camp's older boys were given the Katiaki of befriending Tom as "an act of unbargaining service." So were his cabin mates. Slowly, he found "friends" perhaps for the first time in his life. And Tom had the untrammeled joy of winning a sailing race, beating even older boys. As he walked up to get this award at the end of camp, many of those applauding had tears in their eyes. They knew that their acts of unbargaining service had helped to transform Tom into a happy, productive boy.

Could a similar system of ethics be introduced to your community? I think so.

In 1981, former Chief Justice Warren Burger said, "We have virtually eliminated from public schools . . . any effort to teach values of integrity, truth, personal accountability, and respect for others' rights."

"School prayer proponents are right to link today's social ills with the 1962 Supreme Court's prohibition on prayer and in 1963, on Bible reading," says writer Terry Eastland. These exercises promoted "basic morality, and when they were banned, moral education necessarily suffered." However, Congress did not act on President Reagan's proposed voluntary-prayer amendment.

But it should be noted that the inculcation of basic moral values was never outlawed by the Supreme Court. What this means is that Judeo-Christian ethics can be taught right now, as long as the Bible is not cited as the authority. Is that possible? Yes, we just saw it being done with boys aged eight to fifteen at Camp Agawam in Raymond, Maine, as reported above. Basically, the camp's three strategies could be adapted in other camps attended by 7 million kids, by any private school, and even by public schools, if parents, teachers, and administrators cooperated.

First, campers learned a dozen Woodcraft Laws which were really Judeo-Christian ideals toward which everyone was expected to strive. Second, each boy was given a weekly personality goal to work on such as being neater or helping a younger boy learn a particular sport. Finally, there was campwide recognition given to those who achieved either their short-term goals (called Katiakis) or who demonstrated outstanding sportsmanship or service to others.

Now, let's assume we are interested in seeing the introduction of moral values to Cloverleaf Junior High School. The first obvious question is what values? Next, who is to decide? My suggestion is that a committee of Cloverleaf parents and teachers meet with the principal. It might begin by looking at Agawam's Woodcraft Laws, which could be called "Cloverleaf Ideals." These laws, stated above, are just as relevant to kids in school as to kids at camp. At Cloverleaf, additional values dealing with academics would presumably be added such as "Study diligently. Turn in assignments on time. Seek help when needed." Personality goals might be suggested by parents, and worked on by students for each marking period. Recognition for outstanding sportsmanship or service at the end of the year might be rewarded with trophies.

If programs such as this reached school districts and camps across the country, there is no reason our children couldn't learn to be the moral, responsible people they have the potential to be.

A n s w e r **25**

Church Youth Program Demonstrates Love and Commitment

When we moved in 1987 from Connecticut to Bethesda, Maryland, a suburb of Washington, D.C., it was toughest on Tim, our sixteen-year-old. An athlete and a musician, he'd been popular in Connecticut. In our new town he knew only his grandparents. And he had to start his sophomore year before we could move down, as did his older brother, Adam, a college student. They lived temporarily at their grandparents'. "Don't worry," Adam told us. "I'll get him involved in the youth program at Fourth Presbyterian."

Adam had discovered the church's dynamic youth program two summers before when he was an intern on Capitol Hill. However, Tim was decidedly uninterested in religion. So his mother and I prayed for a miracle.

That first Friday he was invited to a football game by Kenny, a sixteen-year-old whose sister knew Adam. On Sunday, Kenny picked Tim up to take him to a Sunday school class for highschoolers. Tim couldn't believe it. There were 150 laughing kids, many of whom reached out to him, showing love. After we moved down, he asked, "Can I go to church on Sunday night? There's a group that meets called Team." Then he joined a church league basketball team (in addition to playing varsity at school). At Christmas, Tim asked if he could have a "good Bible." We were witnessing a miracle.

About a year later Tim went on a two-week mission trip to Santo Domingo where he and ten others helped build a church. Before he left, I asked him to describe the impact of Fourth's youth program.

"I used to feel dragged to church. Now I want to go," he said simply. Though the church was not in our denomination of twenty-five years, we never considered going anywhere but Fourth Presbyterian to support our kids. We found that many parents made a similar switch—because of their kids.

I asked Joe Chilberg, then the minister of youth, what were the principles behind the success that other churches might learn from. "I pour my life into a handful of people, and they each pour their lives into a handful of kids," he said. "I take a few volunteers, disciple them, and they disciple others. Second Timothy 2:2 puts it: 'And the things you have heard me say . . . entrust to reliable men who will also . . . teach others.'

"People often view the Bible as a message book. But it is also a method book. We have a dinner once a week for all the volunteers in our program— thirty or forty people who range in age from nineteen to thirty. They are committed to teach junior and senior high and college students. Most churches try to minister to everyone. We have quite different programs to meet the needs of a greater cross-section."

I went to a "College Alive" night, another ministry at Forth, attended by one hundred that began with slides of the students, who cheered as they saw themselves. Accompanied by the theme music from *The Pink Panther,* a skit followed, in which "Inspector Clouseau" paced up and down behind "Cato," who was quietly reading the Bible. It was one of a series on the deadly sins, envy in this case.

"Cato, I don't know what it is about you, but I envy you. You are at peace. You are in control of yourself." Cato says his secret is that he has accepted Christ. Clouseau looks up. "Jesus, are you out there? I accept you," sparking laughs. Cato: "No, no. You have to admit you are a sinner, and pray with your heart." He then did so.

A deafening Christian rock group played for half an hour, followed by a thoughtful sermon on envy by Joe Chilberg. Small group discussions got everyone involved afterwards. It was a fun but meaningful evening.

Asked what Fourth meant to them, one student said, "I feel loved here." Another admitted that Eric Stewart, twenty-four, who was Clouseau, paid his tuition at a community college when his parents refused to do so. That is love.

Paul Kokulis, a patent attorney known as "Mr. K" to the kids, has shown a different sort of love. He began teaching the Bible when there were two kids and says, "The youth ministry took off when Chuck Miller arrived in 1962. He started TBC (Thursday Breakfast Club) and asked me to cook." Miller is gone, but Mr. K still cooks for up to three hundred kids at 6:30 A.M. on Thursdays. And perhaps a hundred go to Mr. K's home regularly on Friday nights. "It's a nonthreatening place," his wife says modestly. Over the years, they have been role models to thousands—perhaps a hundred of whom are now clergy.

Pete Bowell, thirty, former director of the high school ministry, led the evangelizing at TBC by infusing 150 kids with Scripture at Sunday school and eighty on Sunday night, the "FAT kids—faithful, available, and teachable."

"We pour our lives into them, those willing to care for others," Bowell said. How? These core kids, led by fifteen volunteer staff, have Bible studies in four high schools and are encouraged to bring friends to TBC and share Christ.

Thus, Fourth's formula is love demonstrated, discipled, and shared.

26 A n s w e r

Alternative Gifts Bring Meaning to Christmas Giving

In 1992, just before Christmas, I received a letter signed by national religious leaders that captured my attention. They were promoting a "Campaign to Take Commercialism Out of Christmas."

It started out well, discussing how they were "deeply concerned about the excessive commercialization of Christmas. For far too long we have witnessed the spiritual yield to the commercial. We have seen the spirit of Christmas reduced to a carnival of mass marketing. Consumption has taken on an almost religious quality; malls have become the new shrines of worship."

But the statement's proposed alternatives were

thin: "We call on people of faith to speak out against the overcommercialization of Christmas in our media and malls." Huh? Are we supposed to tell stores to take down the green and red decorations and turn off the Christmas music?

"Let us invest in renewing our own spirits, our relationships, and our natural environment." Too vague for me! I prefer the specifics suggested by Rusty Gilbert, pastor of Rocky Springs Baptist Church in Lisbon, Louisiana. He has concrete, practical alternatives to Christmas commercialism.

"Every Christmas morning I go out and visit shut-ins, the homebound, and anyone who has had a significant loss in their family in the past year. I take my family with me, and we spend time with these people," he told Chip Alford of *The Baptist Press.*

"We've prayed with them and cried with them. I think it is important for families to touch the lives of people that they don't have to touch [during the holidays]."

Gayle Haywood, minister of preschool and children at Brentwood Baptist Church in Tennessee and a mother of three, has involved her girls in Christmas preparations from a young age. One evening is set aside for Christmas decorating—and not just the tree. The centerpiece is a nativity scene, "low enough so the girls can play with it. And as we unwrap the pieces of the nativity scene, we talk about each character. They've broken some of the pieces, but I think it is important for it to be a hands-on thing that they can play with. It helps them learn about the Christmas story."

My wife, Harriet, was very creative with our boys when they were young. Each year they made Christmas presents for grandparents, cousins, and especially for older friends of the family who were living alone. Often they were decorations that could be hung on a tree—a stained-glass cross or star. One year it was a placemat with bright fall leaves. Many of these have survived and hang on our Christmas tree years later.

What about meaningful Christmas gifts? For a spouse or a sibling, consider a gift that can help make Jesus real all year round. Protestants, for example, might give a subscription to *Christianity Today,* a magazine with an excellent blend of analysis and reporting of contemporary Christian issues (800-999-1704). Catholics ought to consider *Our Sunday Visitor* (800-348-2440).

For a parent, focusing on creating a meaningful Christmas should lead to the question "How can I build my family's foundation on a belief in Jesus Christ?" In this secular culture, this is an immense challenge. Television, movies, and music seduce children into a value structure where anything goes. A Southern Baptist named Wes Allen has come up with a solid and immensely practical way to do this, one any family can afford and use, and something that makes a wonderful gift.

He has created a biblical placemat called "Daily Guidelines to Strong and Happy Christian Families." Allen has selected hundreds of Bible verses that pithily state "Things to Do" to build solid marriages and families, and "Things Not To Do" that are harmful. There are guidelines for thirty-one days.

For example, a parent could read guideline number ten if it is the tenth day of the month, which says, "Parents, instead of leading the family with dominance, abuse, or force, lead them with inspiration and example." It then gives three biblical references. One month the parent might read the first reference, 1 Peter 5:2-3, which is about the role of a parent as a shepherd, "eager to serve, not lording it over those entrusted to you, but being examples."

Dad might ask the kids, "Do you think we have been good examples?" A parent who is that vulnerable will be listened to when correcting a child.

Another month on the tenth, he might look up Colossians 3:19 and read, "Husbands, love your wives and do not be harsh with them." He could then ask his wife, "Do you think I have been harsh with you?" If so, they could then discuss it, and he could apologize!

Daily use of the "Daily Guidelines" will indeed build strong and happy families for the truths of Scripture are eternal. What is lacking in many homes is a way to surface issues on which all members of the family can learn from God's Word. What a wonderful Christmas present that could be—to give your family an easy way to study God's plan for them. The cost is $5.95 per mat or $15.00 for four. Write "Thee Family," Box 530444, Austin, Texas 78753.

Strengthen Flunking Schools—or Transfer Out

American public schools are flunking—both academically and morally. They are not teaching the higher-order skills of reasoning and communication that jobs in the twenty-first century will demand, nor are they grounding our children in ethical principles on which they can build successful lives.

Evidence of absolutely declining academic performance can be seen in the plunging Scholastic Aptitude Test (SAT) scores. In 1960, the combined average SAT score was 975 (477 Verbal and 498 Math). By 1992 the combined score had plunged to a dismal 899 (423 Verbal and 476 Math).

What is worse, former Education Secretary William Bennett noted in his "Index of Leading Cultural Indicators" that "the way the SAT is graded has changed. The same person taking the same test and getting the same answers would score eighteen to thirty points higher in 1992 than in 1960." Yet education spending is way up. In 1990 dollars, the U.S. government spent $2,035 per student in 1960 versus $5,247 per student in 1990.

However, there is hope.

Slowly a plan is taking shape to improve the academic quality of public education. It is based on six educational goals agreed to by former President Bush and all fifty governors, led by then-Governor Bill Clinton of Arkansas. But if your children are in junior high or high school, there will probably be no significant academic or moral change before they graduate. As a parent, therefore, you have to make a decision. Do you keep your kids in public schools and fight for a faster renewal where you now live? That's one option examined in this chapter. It is a valid choice—but one with long odds.

Alternatively, you might decide to place your children in a non-public school. If you are Protestant, you ought to consider the burgeoning Christian school movement. If you are Catholic, definitely look at the parochial school system. Both alternative school systems fare better academically than most public schools and at a fraction of the cost of so-called "independent" private schools. Equally important, both Christian and Catholic schools teach Christian values—the moral component missing from most public schools. Related to that is the increasingly controversial issue of *school choice*—whether you as a parent ought to have partial public subsidy to put your kids in a non-public school. While public teacher unions have killed the option in seventeen states, I believe that school choice is absolutely essential to provide the competition public schools need to begin to pay attention to the desires of parents for quality.

America's National Educational Goals

In 1989 the president and all fifty governors set these six goals to be achieved by the year 2000:

- All children in America will start school ready to learn.
- The high school graduation rate will increase to at least 90 percent.
- American students will leave grades four, eight, and twelve having demonstrated competency in challenging subject matter including English, mathematics, science, history, and geography; and every school in America will ensure that all students learn to use their minds well, so they may be prepared for responsible citizenship, further learning, and productive employment in our modern economy.
- U.S. students will be first in the world in science and math achievement.
- Every adult American will be literate and will possess the knowledge and skills necessary to compete in a global economy and exercise the rights and responsibilities of citizenship.
- Every school in America will be free of drugs and violence and will offer a disciplined environment conducive to learning.

Three years after the goals were set, the 1992 National Educational Goals Report documented almost no progress. For example, it reported:

- Almost two-thirds of students who have failed to master the most fundamental mathematics skills by the eighth grade have still not acquired those skills by grade ten.
- Available evidence points to the existence of a significant 'achievement gap' between American students and their counterparts in other industrialized countries. . . . [The deficiencies] may be present as early as first grade. The achievement gap grows as students get older.

The one area of some progress is in dropout rates. According to the U.S. Census in 1970, 75 percent of all Americans had graduated from high school. By 1985 that number had increased to 83 percent, and in 1990, it was 88 percent.

Our Dismal Academic Performance

Answers 27 and 28 relate the dismal performance of U.S. students. Only *5 percent* of high school seniors are prepared for advanced mathematics. Fewer than 5 percent of seventeen-year-old Americans can understand complex writing. Our reassuring testing system is lying to us. When our students are compared with students in other countries, the truth emerges.

One reason we do so poorly is that only 29

percent of American students spent more than two hours a day on homework (compared to 58 percent of Hungarian kids and 55 percent of the French). A fifth of American students watch *five* hours or more of TV every day, compared to only 7 percent of the Swiss and 5 percent of the French.

Realistic Testing Needed

"Yes, but my school district is different," you may be thinking. "We are above average." I call that the Lake Wobegon effect, "where all the children are above average," as Garrison Keillor puts it. Lake Wobegon tests are "norm referenced." They say, in effect, the "norm" for the eighth grade is X. Your child is doing better than the norm; he's at the ninth grade level. You congratulate yourself for having such a bright child and do not push him to stretch for higher academic achievement. Right?

You must understand the two fallacies in this approach. What if the norm for the eighth grade is dismal? To be considered at the ninth grade level one would only have to be a millimeter better. Second, test results are rigged so that almost every school system can tell its parents, "Our kids are scoring above average, according to national achievement tests." If your principal makes such an assertion, ask him to prove it by naming those school districts in the state that are "below average." You probably won't get examples or data to back it up. Why? Educational testing is virtually fraudulent when community results are compared to national norms, as your principal knows. A physician in West Virginia named Dr. Jon J. Cannell found shocking evidence of the scam. Read Answer 27 to see what happened when he, as a concerned citizen, began asking questions of his school system. You could become the Dr. Cannell of your town!

Fortunately, the National Assessment of Educational Progress (NAEP) is an honest test, one which measures how much students know, using criteria agreed to in advance by teachers in a given subject on what students at a given age ought to know and be able to achieve. As Answer 28 reports, NAEP results are horrifying. Would you believe that only 4 percent of high school seniors in your community can write a persuasive letter to apply for a job?

NAEP was set up by Congress, and is the "only nationally representative and continuing assessment of what American students know and can do in various subject areas." It gathers its data by testing a sample of students, not every student. All of its reports provide only a *national* measure of performance, with the one exception of the 1990 Math Report Card, which has state-by-state data.

Answer 28 argues that parents ought to ask to use NAEP tests to measure the quality (or lack of it) in *their* schools. "This kind of consumer information is absolutely essential for parents in making choices," says the former Under Secretary of Education Ted Sanders. However, that is what the school boards and superintendents *don't* want parents to do. The column makes some suggestions on how parents might fight the system.

Here's one more idea. Simply ask for a copy of the executive summary of "The State of Mathematics Achievement," 1993. Write the Education Information Branch, Office of Educational Research and Improvement, U.S. Department of Education, 555 New Jersey Ave. NW, Washington, D.C. 20208-5641.

High Standards at Home

If your child is in public school, the most important contribution you can make is to set high standards at home. In his final State of the Union Address, in January 1992, George Bush said he met with a group of America's mayors: "Every one of them, Republican and Democrat, agreed on one thing: that the major cause of the problems of the cities is the dissolution of the family." As a parent, *seize control* of your home, if you want your kids to achieve. Answer 29 suggests six steps, beginning with "Turn off the TV."

Carl F. H. Henry, the noted evangelical scholar and the first editor of *Christianity Today,* noted in a recent sermon that the New Testament commands us to meditate upon "whatever is true, whatever is noble, whatever is right, whatever is pure, whatever is lovely, whatever is admirable" (Phil. 4:8). He looked up from his text and added, "If he were here today, would Jesus spend his time watching soaps?"

Instead of allowing our kids to watch TV, my wife took our boys to the library every week to check out books. In Adam's first grade, the teacher held a contest to see who could read the most books in a year. Adam read a thousand. They were mostly small books that a first grader would read. But he listed every title. He won the prize. More important, he learned he could achieve academically.

The other five steps in Answer 29 are equally important.

Religion in Public Schools

Answer 30 provides evidence of the discrimination against the very concept of religion in public schools. One review of sixty textbooks used by 88 percent of Alabama children in grades one through four found "not one word referring to any religious activity." I praise a judge for removing these books from Alabama's schools. Later in the column I cite some wonderful winds of change that began blowing in 1988: the decision to prepare new materials that would give space to the importance of religion in the nation's history. These materials are now available. They have been adopted in Georgia and California, and you can write for details to show to your own school board. More information and an address are in Answer 30.

Expand School Choice

Answer 31 puts a spotlight on a moderate reform that would give parents more choice *within* a public school system—an innovation that Arkansas was pioneering along with New York City several years ago. In East Harlem, when parents could choose between twenty-three different public schools, *all* of the schools saw dramatic improvements due to the competition: two-thirds of students are now "above grade level" or four times the percentage of 1982. This competition *within* the public system is the approach President Clinton favors today.

The Alternative of Religious Schools

However, many parents want more than a choice between public schools. Millions are pulling their kids out of public schools and putting them in religious schools. For a century, Catholics have sacrificed to build a Catholic school system that was educating 5 million students a generation ago. Those numbers have dropped in half as unpaid nuns have retired and have been replaced by teachers whose salaries have to be within striking distance of those in public schools. Tuition has risen sharply—more than many parents of modest means could afford.

Meanwhile, there has been a boom in Protestant schools, usually called "Christian schools." As Answer 32 reports, the numbers doubled from five thousand to ten thousand schools just between 1978 and 1983. Another five thousand schools have opened in the last decade. Altogether, in the fall of 1992 there were 2.6 million students in Catholic schools and 1.6 million in Christian schools. Though both systems spend much less per pupil than the public systems, their students are often two grade levels ahead of their public-school counterparts. For example, New York parochial schools spent only $1,735 per student in a recent year when the city spent $7,107. Yet 99 percent of those in Catholic schools graduated, versus only 38 percent of the public competition! One contributing factor: the Catholics had only 33 administrators to oversee a system for 110,000 kids, while the city staggered under 3,930 administrators for 956,000 students.

Religious schools have become so successful that an attempt was made in 1992 to have Californians vote on an initiative that would have given every student attending a non-public school a grant of $2,600, half the public average cost of $5,200. Of course, teachers' unions fought it, and it failed to gather enough signatures to earn a place on the 1992 ballot. Similar efforts have failed in seventeen states. However, the idea is gaining respectability. It will surface again. See Answer 33 for more information.

If parents are to take their kids back from the world of low academic achievement and violence in so many public schools, they will have to sacrifice financially. They will have to work hard. But there *is* hope. There *are* ways to give our children good education, if we are willing to get involved.

27 *A n s w e r*

Concerned Citizen
Challenges Standardized Testing

You've probably never heard of Dr. John J. Cannell, a physician. But in 1987, he discovered a scandal in American education that appears uglier today because little has been done about it. But he did spark reform.

He found that forty-eight of fifty states claim that their students are "above national average" in achievement. Obviously, that's impossible. Half of the nation's students must be below the national average, and half above.

Dr. Cannell, who now lives in New Mexico, had a general practice in West Virginia in 1987 when he noticed that many of his teenage patients had problems associated with low self-esteem—depression, drug use, and pregnancy. As part of his analysis, he routinely gave them "grade level testing," and found they were often four years behind in grade level.

But when he called the local schools about the kids, "school officials told me that on standardized tests, the kids were 'above the national average.' It happened again and again. I was confused," he recalls.

Then he got suspicious. As head of "Friends for Education," he wrote West Virginia's Department of Education and got a press release stating that the state's students as a whole were "above national average." Having lived in other states, he found West Virginia's claim "unbelievable."

If West Virginia is above the national average, who is below? I bet all claim to be above average, he thought.

He got his X-ray technician to write to every state. Sure enough, even Georgia and South Carolina—poor states like West Virginia—were above average. Arkansas was reluctant to respond, until Cannell's technician said, "I'm thinking of moving to Arkansas; I want to know if the schools are any good." Soon a glossy brochure arrived with a statement that, according to nationally standardized tests, Arkansas students were above average too.

He found that ten states do not have statewide tests, but within them, individual cities use the Metropolitan Achievement Test. And New York City, Boston, and even East St. Louis students were all "above average."

Dr. Cannell called the U.S. Department of Education and asked about such supposedly "nationally standardized tests" as the California and Iowa Achievement Tests that are widely quoted to prove educational quality.

"Those tests are phony," Cannell was told.

"What do you mean, 'phony?'" he asked. "They are standardized tests."

"No one verifies them," he was told. Indeed, they are published as for profit ventures by textbook publishers, like McGraw-Hill, which does the California Achievement Test.

He called McGraw-Hill, saying he was "Superintendent Smith" in a New Jersey school system interested in the California test. "Within minutes, they guaranteed me that my kids would test above average and that the scores would go up every year.

"'Every year?' I asked.

"'It's not a problem,' said McGraw-Hill. 'You're not thinking of changing the questions annually, are you?'"

Cannell quickly realized that if the same tests are given each year, the teachers can teach what the "right" answers are to the questions so students in later years are bound to do better.

Dr. Cannell called the education writer of *The New York Times* to report his findings. He was not interested. But the Associated Press knew a story when it saw it. Soon Dr. Cannell was well-known in educational circles. Then Secretary William Bennett asked him to come speak at a meeting of all of the publishers and education experts about what Bennett called the "Lake Wobegon" effect. Garrison Keillor, host of a national public radio show, often jokes about mythical "Lake Wobegon" where all the women are strong and "all the kids are above average."

What has happened in the years since?

Dr. Cannell has been on "60 Minutes" and "Mac-Neil-Lehrer," but he says "nothing has changed. Friends for Education did another survey two years later of all fifty states; forty-eight states were above average, and 95 percent of school districts claim their students are above average."

But Dr. Cannell's discovery had one key result. The President and state governors set National Educational Goals, which include the goals that "U.S. students will be the first in the world in mathematics and science achievement"; and that "U.S. students will leave grades four, eight, and twelve having demonstrated competence over challenging subject matter."

And, to achieve those goals, they will use "The Nation's Report Card" which *does* measure genuine achievement.

28 *A n s w e r*

NAEP Tests Give Honest Evaluation of School Kids

How would you rate your local public schools? If you said "Good," like most Americans, you are wrong. Dead wrong. If I can prove that, please consider a suggestion here on how you might help.

What percentage of high school seventeen-year-olds are able to write a persuasive letter in applying for a job? 50 percent? 35 percent? 20 percent? 5 percent?

Answer: None of the above. Only 4.1 percent can do so, according to the National Assessment of Educational Progress (NAEP). Here is a typical letter, written by two-thirds of high school juniors or seniors for NAEP:

> I would like to work in a restuarant [sic], or a store. I have worked in restuarants before and it was fun. I also think that it would be fun to be a salesperson because I'm good with people. I want a fun job, because I'm the type of person that does well in a certain thing, when I like what I'm doing and I'd like to do well in my job.

NAEP rates that "adequate"! It seems generous to me. If you were the manager of a department store, would you offer this kid a job? He doesn't seem to know whether he'd prefer flipping hamburgers or selling suits. We only know he wants to have fun. He's "that type of person." Wow.

Reading skills are equally appalling. NAEP's Reading Report Card gives an *A* to only 4.8 percent of seventeen-year-olds who can understand complex writing, which is essential in almost any white collar job today. Only 42 percent can understand simpler writing, such as this newspaper column.

And that figure is a slight increase from the 39 percent who were that "adept" in 1971. But as Albert Shanker, president of the American Federation of Teachers, put it in his column: "At this rate, we'll be in the middle of the next century before we break 50 percent. What does this all mean? And what must we do?" asks Shanker. "It means that when most Americans graduate from high school, they have only the skills they will need if they plan to spend their lives working in a fast-food restaurant or pumping gas. They're not the well-educated, adaptable workforce we'll need to keep the U.S. from declining into a third-rate economic power.

"And they're not citizens who can read, think, talk—and safeguard our democracy." Remember, we are not just talking about ghetto kids. If less than 5 percent can read or write at sophisticated levels, the vast majority of our students are skill-retarded compared to world competitors.

I see one sign of hope, one grave danger, and one step you can take. First, former president Bush and the nation's governors committed themselves at the president's Education Summit to set specific educational goals and outline objective ways to measure accomplishment toward the goals.

Former Education Under Secretary Ted Sanders explains the administration's long-term goal is "to allow parents to choose between and among schools

that their students might attend. That is the corner-
stone of what will actually rebuild American
schools." He points to East Harlem, where parents
can choose between two dozen quite different
schools, and the choice has increased the percentage
of students reading at grade level from 15 to 65 percent. However, he adds, "We need the capacity to
create local assessments of schools. That kind of consumer information is absolutely essential for parents
in making choices."

The danger is that you will never be able to
get a local version of NAEP unless present federal law
is changed. It only permits state-by-state comparisons and prohibits NAEP questions used in local
assessments. The National School Board Association
lobbied for this measure to prevent what it calls
"invidious comparisons" between schools. As you
know, local schools prefer utterly meaningless tests
that purport to show that virtually all students in
their schools are "above average."

That's the kind of mendacity that has lulled parents and taxpayers into believing their schools are
doing a good job. As Al Shanker, president of the
United Federation of Teachers, says, "As long as we
have only national figures to look at, everybody will
continue to think that their own kids are doing OK."

Fortunately, there has been some progress. The
Clinton Administration has submitted legislation
to create a National Educational Standards and
Improvement Council that would have authority to
develop NAEP-like tests—tests that measure what
kids really know and compare it to what they ought

to know at grades four, eight, and twelve. Such tests would give parents information about how their local school and their own kids are really doing. With the support of senators Ted Kennedy (D) and Orrin Hatch (R), the bill has a good chance. Parents, urge your senators and member of congress to pass the bill. Write your local school board, too, and demand an end to the use of Lake Wobegone tests. Demand tests that help us push our kids to prepare for the tough world of global competition.

A n s w e r **29**

You Can Help Your Kids Do Better in Math

In 1988, the U.S. Department of Education released "The Nation's Report Card" on math in a report formally called "The State of Mathematics Achievement." Its conclusions are dismal. But before giving details, I have a question for readers who are parents with children in school: What do you plan to do to at least help your own kids to rise above the dismal norm?

This column will suggest a six-part strategy any parent might take.

But first, you need to know how terrible math achievement really is. Only 14 percent of eighth graders "consistently demonstrated successful performance with problems involving fractions, decimals, percents, and simple algebra—topics generally introduced by the seventh grade," said the Report Card. By twelfth grade, things are no better. All can do third-grade math, but a tenth do not know how to multiply or divide—fifth-grade work!

"Fewer than half the high school seniors (46 percent) demonstrated a consistent grasp of decimals, percents, and simple algebra. And *only five* percent showed an understanding of geometry and algebra that suggested preparedness for the study of relatively advanced mathematics."

What does this mean? "Many students appear to be graduating from high school with little of the mathematics understanding required by the fastest growing occupations or for college work," said the Report Card. "Approximately half the twelfth graders graduating from today's schools appear to have an understanding of mathematics that does not extend much beyond simple problem-solving with whole numbers."

No wonder that of the 10 million high school students who study math each year, "fewer than eight hundred" eventually will earn math doctorates. "And this number has been declining since the 1970s." One concrete cost of this sickening math performance is that much of "college math" is remedial math for poorly prepared students. And business is spending billions in remedial math training according to the Business Roundtable, leaders of Fortune 500 companies.

Yet one of the six "National Education Goals" adopted unanimously by former president Bush and all fifty governors is this: "U.S. students will be first in the world in science and mathematics achievement." But that should provide no comfort for a parent. You should assume the worst, since 95 percent of students aren't learning higher math skills. "Parents are children's first teachers and should remain instrumental to their children's educational success," said the report card on math.

But what if *you* were poor in math. Can you help? *Yes!* Six suggestions:

1. Turn off the TV—"Students who reported watching six hours or more of television per day had substantially lower average mathematics proficiency than their classmates who watched less television," the report card said. When my kids were young, ten to fifteen years ago, they could watch *no* TV during the week, and only a few shows on weekends, such as "Walt Disney." The result: they all played a musical instrument or two, were active in sports, and made good grades.

2. Monitor homework—"Students who did homework daily tended to have a higher proficiency than those who did not do homework." Seems obvious. But millions of parents believe their kids who say, "I have no homework." If they have none, ask their teachers why.

3. Consider parochial schools—The Report Card says, "Fourth and eight graders attending Catholic schools and other private schools had higher proficiency than did students attending public schools, but at grade twelve, the difference was greatly reduced." On average, parochial school students are a grade level higher than public schools in the fourth and eight grades. Why? They offer more discipline and positive values.

4. Do not get divorced—There is a widespread myth in our culture that kids "can adjust" to a

divorce. Do not believe it. Read the book by Judith Wallerstein and Sandra Blakeslee, *Second Chances: Men, Women and Children a Decade after Divorce* (New York: Ticknor & Fields, 1990), based on the only study of the impact of divorce on families during divorce, five, ten, and fifteen years later. Every child suffers, sooner or later—academically, but especially emotionally. Today a quarter of kids live with only one parent.

5. Sit in on your kid's class—If you are unimpressed, sit in on other classes, and demand that your child be moved to a competent teacher.

6. Ask your school to give the National Assessment of Education (NAEP) tests—then your school can have its own "report card." Without this knowledge, you will not become angry enough to demand improvement. Schools will tell you this is impossible. Do not believe it. Write to Education Secretary Richard Riley, who was governor of South Carolina and an early advocate of school reform.

30 *A n s w e r*

Schools Should Teach about Religion

Judge W. Brevard Hand gave joy to many Christians by ordering forty-four textbooks removed from Alabama's public schools in 1987 on two grounds:

First, he said, "These history books discriminate against the very concept of religions, and theistic religions in particular, by omissions so serious that a student learning history from them would not be apprised of relevant facts about America's history."

Even those opposed to removal of the books—

People for the American Way and Paul Kurtz, editor of the Council for Democratic and Secular Humanism's *Free Inquiry* magazine—agree that religion is poorly treated by the books. People for the American Way attorney Ricki Seidman put it this way: "We believe the coverage of religion in the books has to be improved. But the way to do that is not to have the federal court order it."

New York University professor Paul Vitz provides powerful proof of the charge in his book *Censorship: Evidence of Bias in Our Children's Textbooks.* With funds from the National Institute of Education, he examined sixty social studies texts used by 88 percent of America's elementary school children and found:

- "None of the books covering grades one through four contains one word referring to any religious activity in contemporary American life," such as a "child or adult who prayed, or went to church or temple." (Gallup polls show that nine in ten Americans pray and two-thirds are members of churches.)
- There was a little coverage of religion in colonial America for fifth graders, nothing for the last century, and only eleven pictures in fifteen thousand pages.
- No book on modern American social life mentioned the words *marriage, wedding, wife,* or *husband.*

As Mr. Vitz put it in an interview, "If blacks are left out of textbooks, it is racism. If women are left out, it is sexism. If you leave religion out, it is anti-religious prejudice."

The second major conclusion of Judge Hand is more disputed, that "some religious beliefs are so fundamental that the act of denying them will completely undermine that religion . . . [and] result in the affirmance of a contrary belief and result in the establishment of an opposing religion."

That "religion" is secular humanism. Here is how Judge Hand describes it: "Teaching that moral choices are purely personal and can only be based on some autonomous, as yet undiscovered and unfulfilled inner self is a sweeping fundamental belief that must not be promoted by the public schools. The state can, of course, teach the law of the land, which is that each person is responsible for . . . his actions. There is a distinct practical consequence between this fact and the religious belief promoted . . . by saying 'only you can decide what is right or wrong.' With these books, the State of Alabama has overstepped its mark, and must withdraw to perform its proper nonreligious functions."

The case was directly descended from his 1983 ruling dismissing a suit by a parent and children who opposed Alabama's school prayer law. He indicated that if his ruling in favor of prayer were overturned by higher courts, as it was, he would "look again at the record in this case," to give the Supreme Court some of its own medicine by purging secular humanism from public schools. "If this Court is compelled to purge 'God is great, God is good, we thank Him for our daily food' from the classroom, then this

Court must also purge from the classroom those things that serve to teach that salvation is through oneself rather than through a deity," he said.

Thus, there is an element of "getting even" with the Supreme Court, which is childish. Paul Kurtz, the only avowed secular humanist who testified to the court, said, "Secular humanism is a scientific, philosophical, and ethical point of view. It is not a religion. To argue that it is a religion is to distort language. It is like Humpty Dumpty, who said 'up' is 'down.' If secular humanism is a religion, then so is everything—vegetarianism, liberationism, feminism—to which you are committed."

The Rev. John Buchanan, a former congressman from Alabama, who chairs People for the American Way, said of the decision, "I think this is the first time a religion has been defined by its antagonists. It might be called the emperor's new religion—it appears to exist only in the eyes and minds of its beholders. . . . It apparently means anything with which the religious right disagrees."

The case for secular humanism being a religion is weak. But that does not mean there is not a problem with public-school education that teaches nothing about America's religious history, and more important, nothing about the importance of certain values treasured by civilized people of all societies— honesty, courage, selflessness, etc.

If both sides of the argument believe religion should be covered in classrooms, why isn't it? According to Dr. Ernest Boyer, former U.S. Commissioner of Education, "This silence is not because of a conspiracy, but because of a confusion about what such a curriculum should include, and a genuine concern that to discuss religion in the classroom might be viewed as indoctrination, or a violation of the conscience of students, as well as a violation of the fundamental principles of the Constitution." Timidity is the problem—not confusion.

After all, when the Supreme Court invalidated prayer in schools and Bible reading as being an unconstitutional "establishment of religion," it also said, "One's education is not complete without a study of comparative religion or the history of religion and its relationship to the advancement of civilization. . . . The Bible is worthy of study."

Justice Arthur Goldberg wrote, "A vast portion of our people believe in and worship God and many of our legal, political, and personal values derive historically from religious teachings. And so it seems clear to me that the Court would recognize the propriety of . . . the teaching *about* religion as distinguished from the teaching *of* religion."

Fortunately, there is a partial solution, a one-week course (for fifth, eighth, and eleventh grades) on religious liberty in a pluralistic society, developed by noted scholars working with leaders of all major faiths gathered by the Williamsburg Charter Foundation. It has three goals:

1. "To explain the history and significance of the First Amendment Religious Liberty clauses and their decisive contribution to individual and communal liberty and American democracy."

2. "To examine the advantages and responsibili-

ties of living in a modern pluralistic society and to demonstrate how practical dilemmas can be answered in terms of tolerance and mutual respect rather than bigotry and violence."

3. "To deepen each student's appreciation of the principles of religious liberty for peoples of all faiths or none, and so establish a strong civic commitment to the ground rules by which all citizens can contend robustly but civilly over religious differences in public life."

There is absolutely no doubt about the need for such education.

Americans tend to grasp only half of the truth of the First Amendment: "Congress shall make no law respecting an establishment of religion, or prohibiting the free exercise thereof." Do you, like George Bush, think there should be prayer in public schools? Then you only appreciate the last half of the amendment, arguing for the "free exercise" of religion, not seeing that if government requires prayer, it is tending to force faith by establishing religion.

That is particularly offensive to the most rapidly growing segment of the religious population—secularists, people of no religion. In 1962 as in 1952, only 2 percent had no religion. Today 11 percent are secular. And millions of Americans are practicing Buddhists or Muslims. How would you feel if a Buddhist wrote a prayer for Christian children in school?

Pluralism increases tensions. Consider California, which accepts a third of the world's immigration and has a minority majority in its public schools—a mix of Asians, Africans, Latins, and Europeans. In this situation, it is very important that children learn how to "acknowledge our deep and continuing differences over religious beliefs" while recognizing "*how* we debate and not only *what* we debate is critical."

Those quotes are from The Williamsburg Charter that has now been signed by very diverse people—Jimmy Carter, Gerald Ford, Billy Graham, Arie Brower, Elie Wiesel, Phyllis Schlafly, and this writer, to name a few. "This Charter points the way toward effective curriculum development about religion in our schools. . . . The National Education Association is deeply committed to the separation of church and state—to keeping religious training out of our nation's public school—but we are equally committed to teaching about religion and the role of religion throughout history," says former NEA President Mary Hatwood Futrell, a Charter signer.

The curricular materials are now available. Write First Liberty Institute at George Mason University, 4085 University Drive, Fairfax, VA 22030.

31 A n s w e r

Public School Choice Will Improve Education

In one of his first speeches as president, George Bush said, "Further expansion of public school choice is a national imperative."

Arkansas and Iowa paid attention. They became America's second and third states (following the lead of Minnesota) to enact an "Open Enrollment" law, making it possible for a student to transfer from any public school to one in another school district.

In signing the bill, Iowa governor Terry Branstad said the law "represents this state's extra commitment to ensure that our children will be able to successfully compete with the children across the world. It provides parents with the choice of selecting a public school for their children."

It just squeaked through in Arkansas, where a seventeen to seventeen tie in the state senate had to be broken by the lieutenant governor—a circumstance that "just never happens," said then Governor Bill Clinton, its primary advocate. He added, "If people will take advantage of it, it will help a lot of troubled children. And it will give an incentive for all schools to improve."

Ample evidence of that wisdom can be seen in an important book, *Public Schools by Choice* (St. Paul, Minn.: Institute for Learning and Teaching, 1989), edited by educational pioneer Joe Nathan. One chapter puts a spotlight on spectacular academic improvements sparked by increased choice in the unlikely area of Spanish Harlem in Manhattan. "In 1973, the schools ranked thirty-second out of thirty-two districts in reading and mathematics. Less than 16 percent of the students were reading at or above grade level," says Sy Fliegel, the district's former assistant superintendent and architect of its choice plan.

Two-thirds of the area kids are Hispanic; one-third are black. And a third are in families on welfare. With nowhere to go but up, three alternative schools were begun. One was for troublemakers who flourished under a relaxed tutorial system. Another focused on performing arts while also teaching basic skills. It is now one of the largest alternative schools.

Today there are twenty-three alternative schools— often just a cluster of rooms on one floor, where teachers with a common vision run their own emphasis—on sports, environment, science and math, communications and health, and even one on maritime studies. Two or three open annually.

In 1982 parents were given the freedom of choice to send kids to any school. With what result? The percentage of district students reading at or above grade level is 62.6 percent—four times the 1973 percentage. Several hundred white students who live outside Spanish Harlem have transferred to go to its high-quality schools.

"Critics say choice cannot work in inner-city schools because parents lack the necessary education to make informed choices. They are wrong," says Fliegel. A major effort is made to give parents data to compare the schools, such as reading and math scores and high school placements.

Are such data and such choice available in your local schools? Probably not, for this generally is opposed by teachers, school boards, and administrators. Most have worked inside a monopoly all their lives and find competition frightening. They made open enrollment "perhaps the biggest controversy in the history of education in Minnesota," says another writer in Nathan's book. They said students and parents would make bad decisions.

Such mindless opposition prompts some to call for education vouchers, which parents could use for cash to enroll their children in *any* school, public or private. A new coalition has emerged to fight for them called Americans for Educational Choice (940 Westport Plaza, St. Louis, MO 63146). They note that since 1963, average Scholastic Aptitude Test scores have fallen 9 percent while spending increased 351 percent, or 56 percent above inflation. Yet Catholic and private schools, spending half as much per pupil as public schools, have consistently higher achievement rates. They say what's lacking is choice—for parents and students.

Vouchers have begun on an experimental basis in Milwaukee. Students are attending non-public schools with public support in a program that is very popular. Nathan's book outlines an alternative—building choice into public schools. He says, "It permits the freedom educators want and the opportunity students need, while encouraging the dynamism which our public school system requires."

Public Schools by Choice provides evidence that the strategy improves morale, academic achievement, and slashes dropout rates. To learn more, send eight dollars for the book to The Institute for Learning and Teaching, 1852 Pinehurst, St. Paul, MN 55116.

32 *A n s w e r*

Christian Schools Spur Public Schools to Teach Values

"Bible-centered Christian schools are coming into existence at the surprising rate of three new schools a day," said Dr. Paul A. Klienel of the Association of Christian Schools International (ACSI) in 1983. The increase was simply astounding: five thousand Protestant parochial schools in 1978 to about ten thousand in 1983. It has continued growing to about fifteen thousand schools in 1993.

Even so, when Pastor G. L. Johnson of The People's Church in Fresno considered creating one he had "a lot of misgivings and questions. There were so many churches starting schools, I questioned whether their academic standards were what they ought to be."

That concern led Johnson in two directions. First, Johnson—the head of Fresno's largest church, with forty-five hundred people attending each Sunday—asked the pastors of three other evangelical Protestant churches to meet in the pre-dawn hours to pray, plan, and prepare for the school together.

Second, he asked Silas Bartsch, director of teacher training at the small, Mennonite-run Fresno Pacific College, to join the group in brainstorming on how to create "not a school for one church, but a Christian school system for the whole city of Fresno—and one with academic excellence," Johnson recalled.

Bartsch, a former public school superintendent,

was delighted that four churches would join together giving "a strong community base which no single church is equipped to provide. Public schools are responsible to the community they serve. Private schools ought to do the same. That is difficult if a single man or church starts a school," he explained.

The group met monthly for two years before the school opened in 1977 with 135 pupils.

Quality was the keyword in several ways:

- Initially, salaries were competitive with those of public schools. (But average salaries in Christian schools now run a third less than in public schools.)
- Textbooks have been approved by the state of California for secular subjects.
- Teachers are all state-certified and have an average of six years of classroom experience.
- The schools are fully accredited.

More important, the average student is two years ahead of public school counterparts in reading skills, and a year ahead in math achievement. As word of those results spread, Fresno Christian School grew to more than five hundred students in 1982, and then merged with a weak, poorly managed Christian high school. Today there are more than seven hundred students in twelve grades.

The main reason parents send their children to FCS, though, is its spiritual and moral component—introduced as much by teacher role-modeling as by classes.

"We believe the primary source of education is

the role model of another person's life. Education is more than facts and figures and information," said Pastor Roger Whitlow of the Valley Christian Center. "So students need to be exposed to teachers who are living our Christian principles, as well as teaching them the basics."

And, unlike public schools, the Christian school has not cut itself off from the most important book in the world—the Bible. It is studied rigorously in grades seven through twelve in the Fresno system.

What are the results? Former FCS superintendent Joel Wiebe said, "The most frequent comment I hear from parents is that their kids are happy about going to school. They want the discipline, the quality, and being pushed more than they have been pushed."

A more profound effect can be seen in Fresno's public schools, whose former superintendent, John Stremple, says the FCS system "is in the forefront of teaching values—where the society generally feels the public schools have neglected their responsibility. It caused the public schools to deal with the question of values to the extent we can without getting into religion. The board adopted specific values which are to be taught in the curriculum: respect, responsibility, self-worth, justice, love, loyalty, freedom, helping others, integrity."

For example, Fresno's public school board has decreed, "Love is the supreme value. It is an emotion growing out of inner peace which follows a decision to act in response to the needs of others. . . . It is expressed as kindness, generosity, humility, unselfishness, loyalty, consideration, even temperedness, and sincerity." To me, that sounds like a pretty good paraphrase of 1 Corinthians 13.

When I read that to Whitlow, he was thrilled that the Christian schools might be "used by God to prod the public schools back in the direction of giving more training in the moral area. That could spark a spiritual awakening in many students who will want to find out where these things come from. They will learn that it comes from God."

A   n   s   w   e   r *33*

School Choice Gains Popularity

Are the politicians of your state and community talking about raising taxes? Here's an answer from California that will surprise them, maybe avoid a tax hike, and guarantee better education to the kids of your state.

Undoubtedly, you've heard the reports over the last few years about how much better the parochial schools are than the public schools, and how much cheaper they are in doing the job. If not, here is some evidence:

- The National Assessment of Educational Progress reported last year that students in Catholic schools beat public school students by an average of 4.5 percent in math, 4.8 percent in science and 12.5 percent in reading. Using other standardized tests, Catholic kids are a grade ahead.

- Dr. James Coleman, a non-Catholic sociologist from the University of Chicago, has provided similar data for a generation, and adds that the dropout rate in Catholic high schools he studied was less than 4 percent versus 14 percent in public schools.
- Black or Hispanic students are three times as likely to graduate in four years as minority public school kids, says Coleman. And 83 percent of graduates go on to college versus only 52 percent of public school kids.
- New York parochial schools spent only $1,735 per student on average compared to $7,107 in public schools. But an eye-popping 99 percent graduated on time versus only 38 percent of New York public school students.

How are such results possible? Not better salaries. Catholic teachers got only $22,550 but had only eighteen kids in a high school class while public teachers earned $39,136 but had thirty to a class. The fat in public schools is in administration, which employs 3,930 people in New York for 956,000 students versus only 33 in the parochial schools for its 110,000 kids.

So, what has this got to do with taxes? Californians, who often lead the nation in social pioneering (for ill and good), gathered signatures in an attempt to put a "Parental Choice/Scholarships" initiative on the fall 1992 ballot that would give every student a scholarship of $2,600—half of the total public average cost of $5,200—to attend the school of the parents' choice. It could be a new independent public school, a private school, or a parochial one. Or a student could attend any public school, in or out of his neighborhood, and get the full $5,200.

Not surprisingly, Helen Bernstein, president of the United Teachers Los Angeles, said the plan would "rob California's public schools of $1.5 billion." She circulated fliers whose headlines screamed: "The 'Parental Choice/Scholarships' Initiative Isn't Designed to Improve Our Public School System. It's Designed to Destroy It. . . . The initiative doesn't mandate higher educational standards nor does it upgrade educational resources of our children," the flier asserts.

Nonsense. For every child that leaves the public system with a $2,600 scholarship, $2,600 remains in the public schools—without a student to educate. So there are *more* resources per student for those who remain. And will the students who leave get a better public education for the public dollar spent? You'd better believe it.

Consider the Los Angeles Archdiocesan Schools which have a 2 percent dropout rate compared to a 33 percent rate statewide (which includes plenty of great suburban systems). Parochial kids are two grades ahead of the public schools in achievement; yet their tuition is $2,200, not $5,200. Is this achievement because the schools have upper-class white kids? Not at all. Some 43 percent are Hispanic, 10 percent black, 9 percent

Filipino, 5 percent Asian, and, oh yes, 33 percent white Anglos. But the archdiocese has no empty seats in its classrooms, and could not accommodate even five thousand new students—if there were suddenly that many applicants. However, it has raised $70 million as an endowment. If the initiative passed, perhaps it could be tapped to expand the schools.

Certainly Protestant competitors, usually called "Christian schools," would also expand as more parents could afford to pay the tuition.

Assume one million of the five million public school students shifted to non-public schools. That would save state and local governments $2.6 billion. Half of that could be allocated to reduce the deficit or cut local taxes, while half is used to improve public schools. Everyone wins!

No wonder Milton Friedman, Nobel Prize economist, calls it "by far and away the best version I have seen" of educational choice. Former Education Secretary William Bennett adds, "Without giving parents their right to select which school their child attends, the system will not reform itself." Though not enough signatures were gathered to put the issue on California's ballot in 1992, I predict that the issue will surface again in 1994.

This school choice movement is gaining momentum all over the country. In September 1992, a Gallup poll reported that 70 percent of Americans believe government should create a "voucher system" that would allow Americans to "determine where their children should attend school," said Sister Catherine McNamee, president of the National Catholic Education Association, which sponsored the survey. That figure is a sharp increase from only 50 percent supporting parental choice in education in 1991. In fact, public support "has gone up so drastically"—a bigger change than on any other issue, says Gallup vice president Harry Cotugno, that Gallup was surprised and put the question on a second poll, which got almost the same result.

In addition, when Americans were specifically asked if they would be "willing to see some of the tax money now going to the public schools be used to send children to the public, private or parochial school their parent chooses," 61 percent said yes.

However, the results were dismissed as "hilarious" by the Reverend James Dunn, director of the Baptist Joint Committee on Public Affairs. "First, 492 people interviewed were Roman Catholic (out of 1,239), which makes it tilted with double the representation of Catholics in the population. And you have a very thin question: Are you in favor of choice? Are you in favor of heaven? Sure. It was not a question that had any teeth. In eighteen states which had referenda, seventeen of them lost, such as Rhode Island, the most Catholic state, and Massachusetts. That's a poll that means something."

In fact, the issue *was* on the ballot in Colorado

in fall 1992. If it had passed, the constitution would have changed and parents could get a voucher worth 50 percent of the cost of public education, or $2,500 to attend any school. Public schools would keep the other $2,500 without a student to educate.

Dunn was right. Vouchers were defeated in Colorado. After all, only 30,000 of the state's 590,000 students attend religious schools. However, I predict ultimate victory for parental choice of schools. For a clue, take a look at another Gallup question asking for a grade on public schools versus Catholic schools. Some 62 percent give Catholic schools an *A* or *B*, while only 24 percent rank public schools an *A* or *B*. The public's perceptions are correct, as seen by the report from The National Assessment of Educational Progress cited at the top of this article.

What makes these results particularly remarkable is that parochial schools spend so much less than public schools to get this result.

Former President Bush argued, "It's time parents were free to choose the schools their children attend. This approach will create the competitive climate that stimulates excellence." Like every Republican candidate for the White House from Nixon on, Bush has promised but not delivered federal aid if elected. In 1992, he proposed a "GI Bill for children" that would give $1,000 scholarships to five hundred thousand students, one percent of America's 48 million students.

"The proposal is a cynical and cruel move done

for political purposes only," says Rev. Dunn. "It holds forth a false hope when every political realist knows Congress will not pass that legislation." He's right. But Colorado shows that the issue will surface again at the state level.

Take a Stand against Premarital Sex

When I wrote Answer 34 in 1983, I suggested an unusual way to cut the divorce rate: "Teenagers should avoid premarital sex." I smile now as I read that because my opinions haven't changed much. One of the first chapters in my book *Marriage Savers* makes the same point—but with new evidence.

What's the relationship between teen chastity and lifelong marriage? In that column a decade ago, I wrote, "If one can practice sexual restraint before marriage, when the temptation is greatest, it will be much easier to do so afterward. That will create stronger marriages and fewer divorces." It was a reasonable thesis, but it was based on logic, not evidence.

Now there is incontrovertible proof in a study published in the *Journal of Marriage and the Family* (November 1991) by Dr. Joan Kahn and Dr. Kathryn London: "Among white women first married between 1965 and 1985, virgin brides were *less* likely to have dissolved their marriages through separation or divorce than women who had not been virgins at marriage. How much less likely? The numbers are

astonishing. Those who lost their virginity before
marriage are 53 percent to 71 percent more likely to
divorce than those who marry as virgins! Sadly, however, the percentage of women who are virgins when
they marry has dropped from 43 percent in the
1960s to less than 10 percent today. Perhaps that is
due to ignorance. If more teens saw this chart, the
numbers could be reversed:

Divorce Chart

Year Married	Divorced/ Separated Virgins	Divorced/ Separated Nonvirgins	Percent Higher
1980-83	14%	24%	71%
1975-79	21%	34%	62%
1970-74	30%	46%	53%
1965-69	30%	50%	67%

What Kind of Sex Education?

Almost all school systems offer sex education
courses. This seems reasonable, a way to reduce
America's 1.1 million teen pregnancies a year. Ironi-
cally, a Louis Harris poll in 1986 for Planned Parenthood revealed that teens who have taken a sex ed
course have a 50 percent *higher* sexual activity rate
than those who had *no* course. Why? Look at what is
being taught in your local schools. In 1987 Lillian
and Helmuth Krause were shocked to discover what
was taught in chic Westport, Connecticut. Read
what they learned in Answer 35. You may find it

hard to believe. But perhaps it will propel you to your local school district to find out what is being taught there.

Fortunately, there are alternatives to such courses. Answers 36-38 describe three alternatives, courses that not only make a case for sexual abstinence, but also help kids know *how* to say no. After all, even in 1993, nearly half of teenagers are still virgins, says the U.S. Department of Health and Human Services. Therefore, one goal of abstinence-based courses is to give virgins the knowledge, skills, and confidence to remain pure. Another aim is to help nonvirgins achieve "secondary virginity" by remaining chaste, regardless of their previous experience.

Abstinence-based programs really work. The January 1993 Report of the National Commission on America's Urban Families requested by former president Bush, entitled *Families First,* makes this point clear:

> Research suggests that "It may be easier to delay the onset of intercourse than to increase contraceptive practice." Sexuality education courses that emphasize the importance of abstinence seem to result in such a delay— at statistically significant levels. This is compared with traditional sexuality education courses that focus primarily on increasing knowledge about sexuality, on emphasizing the risk and the consequences of pregnancy, or on values clarification.

Sex Respect (Answer 36). Sex Respect is unique because, in addition to the student text, there is a Parent's Guide to help a mother or father discuss this sensitive issue with the teenager. There is also a special Teacher's Guide to help teachers and parents speak with one voice, making a case for abstinence. There are ideas for teachers on how, for example, to do role playing to teach students how to handle the "lines" they'll hear: "You would, if you loved me." Answer: "If you loved me, you would not ask!" Answer 36 offers proof that the course changes attitudes. But what is the long-range impact of Sex Respect? A 1992 study by Dr. Stan Weed, president of the Institute for Research and Evaluation in Salt Lake City, is particularly encouraging: "After two years, those taking Sex Respect in junior high had pregnancy rates that were half of those students not in the programs but attending the same schools."

While Sex Respect is in several thousand high schools, it is getting very few headlines. What is getting wide coverage is New York's answer to teen sex: handing out condoms. On the night the city's board of education voted four to three "to take a plunge into darkness," refusing parents the right to prevent their children from getting the condoms, I wrote a column citing a study that proves that handing out condoms for five years in six cities did *nothing* to reduce teen pregnancy. Sadly, the promise of "safe sex" induces a higher percentage of teens to become sexually active—more than offsetting any reduction of pregnancies due to condom use. In San

Francisco, for example, 25 percent more students lost their virginity after condom handouts, and there was a 25 percent increase in student pregnancies. That's why I believe that giving condoms to teens is like pouring gasoline on fire.

Postponing Sexual Involvement (Answer 37). Washington, D.C., schools soon decided to give out condoms too. That move sparked a debate on "Nightline" between Washington mayor Sharon Pratt Kelly, who enthusiastically backs condom handouts, and former Education Secretary William Bennett, who thinks giving out free condoms makes no more sense than showing hard-core porn in English class. What is the alternative? I describe an abstinence-based program that is working well in inner-city schools, "Postponing Sexual Involvement."

PSI differs from Sex Respect in that it is *not* taught by teachers. Instead, eighth graders hear from eleventh and twelfth graders—role models a few years older who are trained to present facts, identify pressures, and teach assertiveness skills in a way no teacher could. Slightly older teens show it is cool to say no. Most teens taking the course decide at least to postpone becoming sexually active. But what matters is long-term impact, and the most recent data is very encouraging. See if PSI would work well in your kids' school.

Why Wait? (Answer 38). Both Sex Respect and PSI are designed to be used in public schools. That means by definition that they are missing an ingredient that can add authority and power: a clear scriptural perspective. As Paul wrote to the Thessalonians: "God wants you to be holy and pure, and to keep clear of all sexual sin so that each of you will marry in holiness and honor—not in lustful passion as the heathen do, in their ignorance of God and his ways" (1 Thess. 4:3, TLB).

Fortunately, there is a course aimed at church youth that adds the power of Scripture to the abstinence argument of the other courses. It is Josh McDowell's Why Wait? series, based on his experience talking to 8 million high school and college students in person over the last twenty years. Why Wait? is a video series that injects a lot of fun with music, humor, and dramatization. The course is popular; it has been used by sixty thousand churches as of 1992. As I report in Answer 38, Why Wait? is really two video series, one for teens and the other for their parents. As one father told me, "It built a bridge between me and my daughter which did not exist before." How successful is Why Wait? Alas, its creators have not commissioned an independent study of its effectiveness, which is hard to understand given its high sales. But the pastors, parents, and kids I've talked with give it high marks.

Clean Teens (Answer 39). In 1987 I was asked to speak to an anti-pornography rally in Modesto, California, by an activist there named Harry Kullijian. He had organized a group called CLEAN (Citizens Leading Effective Action Now) and enlisted an astonishing two thousand members, who all turned out at the rally. After I finished, a young man walked up to Harry Kullijian and me. He said, "I'm Kirk McCall, a college student here." A woman watched Kirk as he began to talk animatedly with me about the need for purity among teenagers. She tugged at Harry's sleeve and said, "You forgot something."

Harry said, "What?"

She replied, "Clean Teens."

Harry spun around, put his hand on Kirk's shoulder, and said, "We're going to create Clean Teens, and you're going to be the president!"

Kirk, then aged eighteen, agreed, saying: "We *do* need an organization of *teens talking to teens* about the need for sexual purity."

That was the genesis of the group described in Answer 39. First published in 1987, this column generated hundreds of letters from teens around the country who wanted to start their own Clean Teens organization. That motivated Kirk, and later his successors, to create a video that tells the stories of eleven Modesto teenagers who struggled to deal with sexual pressures.

One of those teens, Angie Holroyd, tells of "searching for security and searching for love," which she thought she found through sex. "I couldn't differentiate physical love from emotional love," she says on the video. Her confusion led to pregnancy, abortion, and contracting a sexually transmitted disease (STD). "It made me realize death is real in sex," she says movingly. (Indeed,

STDs infect 3 million teens a year. Each year they render one hundred thousand women infertile! And at least ten thousand teens contract AIDS. At the University of Texas, one student out of a hundred coming to a health center carries the deadly disease, according to Focus on the Family.)

Clean Teens has also created an eight-lesson course that teens in any community could offer to other teens. It's called "Warning: Safe Sex May be Hazardous to Your Life." It includes a manual on organizing a local chapter.

How effective is Clean Teens? Their leaders have spoken to dozens of schools and church youth groups, adding personal testimony to what could be seen on the video. Sadly, Clean Teens doesn't exist in Modesto any more. Kirk trained a second generation of teens to take on the leadership, but a "generation" to a teenager is two years. By the third "generation," four years after Kirk started the group, the original enthusiasm burned out. (Kirk is now married and is studying at a seminary.)

However, the video and materials have been sent out to hundreds of communities requesting them, and they are still available from the address given in Answer 39. I suggest that adults interested in helping teens assume leadership also write to Postponing Sexual Involvement (See Answer 37) to learn how to train eleventh and twelfth graders to work with eighth graders. Such adult oversight is essential for a program's continuity. Clean Teen materials could be an effective supplement to the PSI course, which also uses a video.

When a Teen Gets Pregnant

Every year one million teenagers get pregnant. Of that number, an estimated 13 percent have a miscarriage. What should the rest of the pregnant teens do? In America, debate polarizes around two options:

- Get an abortion. There were 407,000 teen abortions and 134,000 teen miscarriages in 1988.
- Have the baby and keep it. There were 489,000 births to teens in 1988 and 518,000 in 1989, of which 349,000 were to unwed teenagers. (Two-thirds of all black babies and a fifth of white ones are born out of wedlock.)

Neither option is constructive, in my view. A few women die each year from botched abortions. A larger number (no one knows how many) become infertile. Many more suffer psychological trauma for years. And a precious life is lost.

On the other hand, to have a baby out of wedlock is a ticket to welfare and poverty for most young women, particularly teenagers. Half of those now on welfare had their first child as a teenager. Few ever marry. "Even controlling for factors such as race and income, children from single-parent families are more than two and a half times as likely to drop out of school as those living with their own parents," reports *Families First*. "Father absence is an important predictor of problems such as juvenile crime, poor school performance, and adolescent pregnancy."

In fact, the first paragraph of the Bush Commission report *Families First* makes this stark point:

> Every child needs the love and provision of his or her mother and father. Compelling evidence demonstrates that the stable and loving two-parent home provides the healthiest environment for children, and is an irreplaceable foundation for long-term societal success.

There is a way to save babies of teenagers, a way that can truly liberate both mother and child: adoption. It is the neglected option, chosen by only twenty-five thousand of the million mothers of out-of-wedlock children in 1992. This is not because there are no homes willing to take the children. More than a million couples want to adopt babies but can't find any. About ten thousand couples a year travel to Korea, Romania, Russia, or Peru to adopt a child.

Why are so few babies adopted? In Answer 40, I write, "There is a scandal in the pro-life movement. Almost none of the babies being saved from abortion are being given up for adoption." Counselors in crisis pregnancy centers, anxious to save the baby, tell women, "Keep the baby. You can make it. We will help." Yet the help usually stops at the baby's birth. The future is usually bleak for the young unmarried women who choose to give birth and keep their babies.

It is time for the pro-life movement to be as pro-life after birth as it is before. Crisis pregnancy centers should regularly create the opportunity for unmarried women to meet with parents who have adopted a child, with adults who were adopted as children, with mothers who placed children for adoption years ago and are glad they did, and with couples in solid marriages who want to adopt. It is not enough to hand a woman a phone number of an adoption agency and consider the task completed.

There is an antiadoption bias in our culture. It is fed by heart-rending media stories of adult children looking for their "natural mother." In real life, such mothers and children rarely want to see each other. Why doesn't the media tell happy adoption stories, such as the adoption of Gerald Ford as a baby?

The pro-choice people rarely present the adoption option. Why not? It is a *choice*. President Bill Clinton said, "I believe abortion should be safe, legal, and rare." I wrote, "If he believes that, why doesn't he call a White House Conference on Adoption?" He could call for a "pro-life, pro-choice truce, with people from both sides working together to give babies and their mothers a better future."

The Homosexual Option

For some teenagers, the temptation is to have sex with someone of the same gender. Homosexual experimentation occurs more often among boys than girls. However, it is only one fifth as prevalent as the media constantly claim, as Answer 41 shows. And homosexual behavior is infinitely more changeable than the media report. Masters and Johnson, the famous sex therapists, say they can successfully help three-fourths of their patients who want to discontinue homosexual activity. And over a hundred Christian ex-gay groups have helped five thousand men and women out of this life-style by using mentoring techniques similar to those of Alcoholics Anonymous, but with a strong focus on confession, healing, Jesus, and prayer.

Answer 42 tells how Anthony Falzarano, a former male prostitute who had four hundred sexual partners, has been completely healed, has married, is a father, and now leads an ex-gay group, Transformation, in Washington, D.C.

President Clinton is leading the nation in a different direction with his efforts to lift the ban on homosexuals in the military. What's wrong with lifting the discrimination against gays? Solid medical evidence shows that even gays *without AIDS* die at the average age of forty-one! Rather than glamorizing the deadly homosexual choice, our government and our churches should do all in their power to help them choose health and life instead.

Sadly, Christians have failed to show the compassion to homosexuals that Jesus showed to the woman who committed adultery. He stood up to those who were ready to stone her, saying, "Whoever is without sin, cast the first stone." When they all walked away, he told the woman, "Go, and sin no more" (John 8:3-11). Jesus loved the sinner while hating the sin. So must we.

If your teen has homosexual temptations—or if you know someone else who does—don't condemn him as a person. Don't quote Scripture at him, threaten him, or shut him out of your life. Rather, give him your love and support and the phone number of Exodus, a national umbrella group of ex-gay ministries, all of which are supervised by local churches. The phone number is in Answer 42, and I will give it again here because it is so important: (415) 454-1017. Exodus can refer readers to the nearest group like Transformation.

A n s w e r **34**

Premarital Sex Is a Factor in Divorce

One couple of every two who get married will experience divorce. But nowhere amidst the tales of custody battles and the failure of two-thirds of divorced fathers to provide child support is there a single suggestion on what might be done to reduce the number of divorces.

I'd like to suggest one answer based on traditional Judeo-Christian values: Teenagers should avoid premarital sex. To even suggest it in today's hedonistic culture, where *Penthouse* and *Playboy* magazines have a far more powerful influence than the Scriptures, may seem hopelessly naive or outdated.

But consider what Hugh Hefner, the founder of *Playboy*, once said when television interviewer David Frost asked, "Hugh, now that you've got everything that a man could possibly want—all the fame, and success, and women—what would you like now?" Hefner replied, "David, I'd give everything I own to find true love." What he seemed to be saying was that sex is not the route to true love.

The Bible agrees. Consider Genesis 2:24, "For this reason a man will leave his father and mother and be united to his wife, and they will become one flesh." In his superb book, *Dating: Guidelines from the Bible* (Grand Rapids: Baker, 1979), Scott Kirby makes two points about that passage: "God is very positive toward sex. Unfortunately, many people think that God has put a hex on sex! It is true that God is down on the misuse of sex [saying] that the only right place for sex is in the marriage relationship. Notice that in Genesis 2:24 that leaving [one's parents] comes before cleaving. Marriage comes before sex."

But most people disagree. According to the Gallup poll, two-thirds of Americans don't believe it is wrong to have sexual relations before marriage.

And what are the consequences? An estimated 20 million Americans now suffer from an incurable venereal disease called genital herpes. A *Time* cover story on the disease said its rapid spread is "delivering a numbing blow to the one-night stand. The herpes counterrevolution may be ushering a reluctant, grudging chastity back into fashion." (And do we even need to mention the AIDS plague?)

Unfortunately, the evidence points in the opposite direction. Four out of ten teenage girls become pregnant despite the wide availability of contraceptives. And illegitimacy has tripled despite a tripling of abortions ever since they were made legal. Tens of millions of Americans are thus paying a high price for sexual promiscuity, which they often refer to as love.

But what about premarital sex when it is between two people who feel they "love" one another, who practice birth control? Scott Kirby says that young people confuse infatuation, an excited feeling, with love, which involves a commitment. "Infatuation is just love of emotion. Real love, though, is love of devotion. Only the emotions are affected in infatuation, but in real love, both the emotions and the will are involved."

St. Paul gave this definition in 1 Corinthians 13:4-8, "Love is patient, love is kind. It does not envy, it does not boast, it is not proud. It is not rude, it is not self-seeking, it is not easily angered, it keeps no record of wrongs. Love does not delight in evil but rejoices with the truth. It always protects, always trusts, always hopes, always perseveres. Love never fails."

This sort of love—one of sacrifice—does not come naturally. "At the very point when young love needs God, premarital sex will drive it away," says Rev. Peter Moore, the founder and former director of an organization that works with teenagers in many East Coast private schools called FOCUS (Fellowship of Christians in Universities and Schools, P.O. Box 4609, Vineyard Haven, MA 02568. 508-693-4824). "One has to go—God or premarital sex," he says. Why? "Eros substitutes lust for love. You use the other person rather than care about them. Your attitudes towards the other person are affected negatively." How? "By focusing on the sexual experience outside of marriage, where there is no environment of commitment, the male becomes a con-artist, professing his 'love' for the woman, to get the sex. Meanwhile the girl gives sex to get love. Both are fooling themselves, out of a narcissistic preoccupation with the self, which leads to guilt. This sets the stage for poor relationships in marriage.

"Divorce is the all-too-frequent result.

"But isn't sex a natural feeling? Of course, says C. S. Lewis in his classic little book *Mere Christianity* (Westmont, New Jersey: Barbour & Company, 1985, p. 85). 'The lie consists in the suggestion that any sexual act is also healthy and normal. Now this, on any conceivable view, and quite apart from Christianity, must be nonsense.'"

If one can practice sexual restraint before marriage, when the temptation is greatest, it will be much easier to do so afterward. That will create stronger marriages and fewer divorces.

35 *A n s w e r*

Parents Should Evaluate Sex Education Courses

In a time of AIDS, herpes, and soaring teen pregnancy, sex education is clearly a needed course in public schools. But parents should take a look at the content of the curriculum being offered.

Helmuth and Lillian Krause were so stunned by

Westport, Connecticut's course materials—a book, visuals, and audio tapes—that they joined a review committee and denounced the course at June hearings of the school board: "We are not against sex education . . . but the high school course goes beyond the basic knowledge required to deal with sexuality," Helmuth said. "The pathologic emphasis on homosexuality, bisexuality, and other deviate and perverted sexual acts—presented as coequal with heterosexual normalcy in the resource material—is an offense to a healthy conscience.

"The teaching of human sexuality in its present form appears to be a how-to course in sexual experimentation and exploitation. These manipulative strategies are presented without consideration of partner or consequence, without consideration of right or wrong, and in direct opposition to parental concerns and traditions and to societal standards. Adolescent celibacy is not emphasized as a positive life value to be pursued. Sexual intercourse is not emphasized as belonging in the bonds of marriage. With pandemic proportions of sexually transmitted diseases, children must be challenged to a sense of responsibility and respect toward themselves and society. Premarital celibacy must be idealized again for reasons of self-preservation of this nation," he concluded.

However, the Krauses were outvoted by a vote of twenty-one to two on the review committee and faced overwhelming opposition in two public hearings.

"The most important task we face as parents is

preparing our children for life," said a father. "And a big part of that is giving information that will protect them from harm . . . a knowledge of all the hazards, including that of ignorance. You don't ignore a viper in the jungle just because it is poisonous or ugly or repugnant to your life-style." Westport officials said they were "proud" of the program because it emphasized "the importance of a positive self-image and responsibility for others." And they emphasized that "families uncomfortable with the curriculum may have their children opt out of the sexual portions."

A physician speaking for the town's seven pediatricians said, "We urge you to continue and expand the human sex program. With the rapid spread of AIDS . . . it is imperative they know how to protect their well-being." But a few parents argued it would spark promiscuity, not caution. Lois Roberts, an engineer and mother of an eighteen-year-old, said, "I am shocked at the content of this book." She tried to quote it, but was too embarrassed.

Therefore, Lillian Krause decided the next week to read excerpts and ask school officials to defend them. They refused to answer her questions.

For example, she noted that the system's textbook, *Learning About Sex* by Gary Kelly, said of anal sex (the primary means by which AIDS is spread), "Unless there are special medical problems, when cleanliness and care are observed, there are no special medical dangers associated with anal sexual contact." Then she asked if the book "has given its young readers insufficient and potentially danger-ous information?" Of course it had. She noted that a new edition of the book adds this single sentence to the one about "no special medical dangers." "It is believed the disease AIDS may be spread, a dis-ease that's fatal."

On sex with animals, Kelly writes, "There are no indications that such animal contacts are harmful, except for the obvious danger of poor hygiene, injury by the animal or to the animal, or guilt on the part of the human." Mrs. Krause said, "This appears to give approval to bestiality."

She noted the kids must answer whether they have participated in "circle jerk," and asked offi-cials if they'd describe it and explain why it is asked. "What is the pedagogic relevance and pur-pose of the step-by-step description of masturba-tion, or the insertion of objects in the vagina, or the tasting of semen?"

Finally, Mrs. Krause pointed out that at the end of the course, students must fill out a questionnaire that asks whether the student has performed nine-teen different sexual acts, and if so, age at first expe-rience, how they liked it, and if parents know about it: cunnilingus, intercourse, fellatio, anal sex, group sex, orgasm, same sex experience, etc. "What is the purpose of this type of questioning other than to sat-isfy the course developer's own prurient curiosity and supposed success of the course?" she asked. Even parents backing it winced or smiled nervously.

But there were no public answers to the questions. Later, however, School Board Chairman Dorothy

Lyne told me, "We did not approve that book. It was done ten years ago. We are reconsidering the course."

Seven years later, the book is still being used.

36 *A n s w e r*

"Sex Respect" Teaches Abstinence

New York City's board of education decided parents will *not* be able to keep their children from getting free condoms handed out by the schools. As a result of this radical plan, New York schools give condoms upon request ultimately to 260,000 students in 120 city high schools—more than have been given out in all of the nation's experimental "school based clinics" put together. And all other cities require parental consent.

As with "sex education," condoms are supposed to keep teens from getting AIDS or pregnant. "This has been tried in other cities: Dallas, St. Paul, San Francisco, and Baltimore. It didn't work in any of those cities," Jack Hartigan, a lawyer for the Coalition of Concerned Clergy and Parents, told the board.

Evidence? A study looked at five years of experience in six cities: Dallas; Gary, Indiana; San Francisco; Muskegon, Michigan; Jackson, Mississippi; and Quincy, Florida, and concluded, "None of the clinics had a statistically significant effect on schoolwide pregnancy rates." Says who? A skeptical conservative? No. That was published in *Family Planning Perspectives,* a magazine of Alan Guttmacher Institute, of Planned Parenthood, a clinic proponent.

Josh McDowell, who has made a case for chastity to millions of college students in person, spoke during "Safe Sex Week" at the University of North Dakota. He began by saying, "You've been brainwashed! You've had a week of 'safer sex' indoctrination: speakers, experts, videos. . . . You've been encouraged and pressured to use condoms. To top it off you've been given a 'safer sex packet.' But you've been lied to." The crowd was becoming a little indignant. Then he asked, "How many of you know the statistical failure rate of the condom?" Not one hand went up.

For teens, the condom failure rate is 16 percent; the pill is 11 percent. A UCLA study found that the HIV virus leaked through Trojans, made by Carter-Wallace. Schmid's Ramses condoms had to be recalled due to "an unacceptable level of holes and ring tears." And these are the companies giving New York City 450,000 free condoms—a doubtful honor.

An even bigger problem is the moral problem. Catholic Bishop Thomas Daily of the Brooklyn-Queens Diocese, issued a pastoral letter saying, "The program of condom availability within a school tells students that the school believes that extramarital sex is acceptable." It is implying "that promiscuous behavior is an acceptable mode of conduct. A program for teaching young people about the meaning of human sexuality is, in the first instance, the responsibility of the family . . . complimented by the Church, Synagogue, and Mosque. The Public School is not well equipped to teach about human sexuality and indeed is usurping the rights of parents when it takes over this responsibility."

An example of the poorly equipped public school system is in Virginia where a curriculum has been introduced that "teaches situational ethics, where there is not right or wrong," says Alice Tennies, a former teacher who chaired a committee studying the curriculum. She told a meeting of Concerned Women for America that Arlington teachers heard this in a training session: "Assume that you are in Hawaii without your partner. Pretend these pieces of paper are keys. Trade keys with someone you'd like to spend the night with."

"Teachers were role-playing adultery!" exclaimed Mrs. Tennies.

But a million pregnant teens show that families and churches are also failing in their responsibility to teach responsible sexual behavior. Illegitimacy quadrupled since 1960 (224,000 a year to 1,165,000 in 1990), and divorce and abortion rates have tripled. Therefore, if the school must assume some responsibility, it should do so in a moral way that reduces teen promiscuity. The assumption behind most sex education and making contraceptives available is that they will reduce pregnancy. In fact, they are gasoline poured on the fire of lust. Chuck Colson has said that the greatest myth of the twentieth century is that people are good. We aren't.

But there is an alternative. It assumes that we are a sinful people who can be redeemed—that our ethical standards can be raised. "Sex Respect" is a curriculum that changes teen attitudes toward sex. It makes a persuasive case for teenage sexual abstinence. Now in over a thousand public schools, Sex

Respect reveals the harmful emotional, psychological, and physical consequences of teen sexual activity. It shows that abstinence gives freedom to mature, develop confidence, make career plans, while raising self-esteem and creating a capacity to be faithful to a future spouse, and disassociating sex with guilt, fear, and shame.

Its author, Coleen Kelly Mast, says that sex ed courses "are too narrow, focusing only on the physical, saying if you get rid of the physical consequences of premarital sex (via contraceptives or abortion), all will be OK. That is a lie. . . . There are serious emotional and physical effects. Even adults have difficulty getting over a sexual relationship. Teens are being taught that they can act on any impulse and not have to face the consequences. How can we create a healthy society when its citizens have not learned self-control?" In a Parent's Guide, a syllabus written to spark family dialogue, she says a goal is to "save their teens the heartaches of broken love affairs, the burden of teenage pregnancy, and the pain and suffering caused by sexually transmitted diseases."

The first chapter for teens begins, "Just as we had to learn to crawl to stand, and to balance before we could walk, so we have to learn about the mental, spiritual, and emotional parts of our sexuality before we are mature enough to handle the physical part, or sexual intercourse. . . . Boys tend to use love to get sex. Girls tend to use sex to get love. Unlike animals that have no choice but to mate when they are in heat (fertile), we humans can *think* before we act on our sexual drive. . . . True freedom is not the same as impulsiveness. Freedom is really self-control."

It even teaches how to deal with lines: "If you loved me, you would." Response: "If you loved me, you wouldn't ask."

Mrs. Mast says, "Most teens, given clear-cut reasons to say no to premarital sexual activity, will jump at the chance to escape." Evidence: Some 1,841 students were questioned before and after the course in six Midwestern states. Only 20 percent of teens felt they could "always" control their sexual urges before the course. That doubled to 39 percent afterwards. Before the course, only a third saw any benefit for sexually active teens to stop having sex. After Sex Respect, 59 percent felt that way!

As a result of reporting these findings, I was invited by Dr. Robert Campbell of the First Presbyterian Church of Washington, Pennsylvania, to discuss Sex Respect with a panel of students, educators, and parents. At first, the students were quiet. I asked them to describe their sex ed course. "Plumbing," said one.

"Are values taught?" I asked.

"No. They don't say anything that deals with the world—only AIDS, not other sexually transmitted diseases, and nothing on sexual abstinence," said Erin Leslie, fifteen. "Sex Respect is a good idea."

Jim Hanna, principal of a junior high agreed, but said, "We need a message from the community of what it wants us to do, and will support."

John, age seventeen, said, "The aim of a lot of

guys is conquering. They want to be free to do what they want. It would be good to teach values."

The parents initially were noncommittal. One noted how much sexual promiscuity is promoted by television, wondering how a program could help. I cited the data that twice as many kids felt they could control their sexuality afterwards.

Finally, Dr. David Leslie, a gynecologist, spoke up: "In twenty years, this is the best program I have ever seen. Others are harmful. Sex Respect could really help. Let's get it in the schools."

All agreed and formed a committee to fight for it.

An independent evaluation of Sex Respect by the Institute for Research and Evaluation found that before taking the course, 36 percent of students said teen intercourse is acceptable if no pregnancy results. Only 18 percent agreed afterwards. And follow-up a year later found that Sex Respect grads were half as likely to be sexually active as other teens. Now that's a program that works.

If you would like to find out more about Sex Respect, I urge you to send $8.95 for a copy of *Sex Respect Parent Guide* to Respect, Inc., P.O. Box 349-M, Bradley, IL 60915.

A   n   s   w   e   r **37**

PSI Program
Reduces Teen Sexual Activity

In considering the decision by Washington, D.C., schools to hand out condoms to students, I remembered a brief speech I heard on Capitol Hill on May 7, 1992, the National Day of Prayer, by Dr. James

Dobson, host of radio's "Focus on the Family": "We are involved in a civil war of values that is a fight to the death between two incompatible worlds that will not mesh together. At the core of the difference is who God is, whether He lives or whether He does not."

One side holds Judeo-Christian values:

> God *is* . . . the origin of everything good— immutable truths passed down to every generation such as sexual fidelity between spouses in lifelong marriage, the value of every person, whether an unborn child or the aged who cannot produce anything but still has worth because God created that person. That we are "endowed with certain inalienable rights" that came from God was an assumption of our forefathers.

On the other side are those who assume that "there is no God—a value system that makes up rules as you go along. What seems right *is* right. Decisions on public policy are made by opinion polls," said Dobson. "These two world views are on a collision course. And both sides know, especially secular humanists, that children are the prize to the winner."

The collision was nowhere more evident than a debate on ABC's "Nightline" about giving out condoms to students. Guests on the show were Washington, D.C. mayor Sharon Pratt Kelly and former education secretary William Bennett.

Kelly: "AIDS is spreading faster in the District of Columbia than in any city. Teenagers are at risk. An epidemic demands drastic action."

Bennett: "If you have a cancer, you don't switch from Camels to a filter cigarette. You give up smoking. . . . To say you are teaching sexual responsibility and handing them condoms is like teaching them about fiscal responsibility and handing them a hundred dollar bill."

Kelly: "This is a public health issue. But it is an issue that kills. Seventy-five percent of tenth graders are already sexually active and 40 percent have had four or more partners. We have to do what's necessary to urge them to abstain, but make condoms available to those who won't."

Bennett: "Our sons and daughters are made in our image and in the image of God. We do not have to surrender. You know that in our drug fight, we did not surrender and drug use is on the way down."

Kelly claimed she wasn't surrendering, because "health care professionals are educating our children" along with guidance counselors.

Bennett asked, "Is there a role for parents to excuse them from this?" The mayor merely said they would be notified: "Look realistically at what's happening. It's obvious they're not listening to their parents. Young people are dying, innocent young people."

Innocent? Bennett countered that "more children will be at risk and more will die" by handing them condoms. Why? "According to Planned Parenthood, the failure rate of condoms is 16 percent in preventing pregnancy, and you can get pregnant only one time a month. HIV can be caught any time of the month. The failure rate in preventing AIDS is 36 percent."

Unfortunately, Bennett did not put a spotlight on an alternative strategy that can work with inner city youth: "Postponing Sexual Involvement," which was invented in Atlanta by Dr. Marion Howard, director of Teen Services at Grady Memorial Hospital, which serves poor blacks.

PSI is taught not by teachers or health professionals, but by eleventh and twelfth graders who are trained to use positive peer pressure with eighth graders. Why? Howard found that "simply providing young teenagers with information was not effective in changing sexual behavior." What made a difference was "role models," teens slightly older than those being given the course who present factual data, identify pressures, teach assertiveness skills, and discuss problem situations. A key focus, based on a survey of more than a thousand sexually active girls "is what 84 percent of them most want to know: 'how to say no without hurting the other person's feelings.'"

To measure the effects of PSI, 536 low-income minority students were interviewed—395 who took the course and 141 kids in schools without it.

The astounding result: "By the end of the eighth grade, students who had not had the program were as much as five times more likely to have begun having sex than were those who had the

program." Those eighth graders have now graduated from high school and have had a one-third
reduction in pregnancies compared to those who
did not take the one week course.

To learn more, write Emory/Grady Teen Services
Program, Box 26158, Grady Memorial Hospital,
Atlanta, GA 30335.

A   n   s   w   e   r   **38**

"Why Wait?" Gives Teens Reasons to Wait for Sex

Many churches and synagogues in America are
failing to teach biblical sexual ethics. Surely Scripture is clear: "It is God's will that you should be
sanctified: that you should avoid sexual immorality; that each of you should learn to control his
own body in a way that is holy and honorable,
not in passionate lust like the heathen" (1 Thess.
4:3; See also Prov. 7).

Yet 1.1 million teenagers get pregnant annually—
seven times the per capita rate of Denmark, where
church attendance is a quarter of that of the
United States. Tragedy results. Half will have abortions, and half will have illegitimate babies.

And where is the church? Scandalously silent, all
too often. The "Teen Sex Survey in the Evangelical
Church," commissioned by the Josh McDowell
Ministry in such conservative denominations as
the Church of the Nazarene and the Lutheran
Church—Missouri Synod, found that three-fourths
of church youth learned little or nothing about sex
from their church. Yet four-fifths of these church

kids are members of youth groups. What are they teaching? Some 43 percent of church youth aged eighteen have had sexual relations. That's only slightly less sexual activity than secular kids.

Fortunately, there is an answer: a program called "Why Wait?" that already has been adopted by ten denominations and used by sixty thousand local churches.

"The Why Wait? campaign could well be one of the most significant things that has happened in our country for decades," say Vonette and Bill Bright of Campus Crusade for Christ. It involves a videotape series for teens, "NO! The Positive Answer," and one for parents, "How to Help Your Child Say NO to Sexual Pressure."

In one tape, McDowell, who has spoken in person to 8 million students, talks about why the word *no* has "two positive elements—to protect you and provide for you." He asks students to imagine that they trained for years as swimmers and made it to the Olympics. But when they show up for the ultimate race, the swimmers are lined up on all four sides of the pool.

"All jump in!" they are told. "It's not a race, but a demolition derby!" That's why pools are divided into lanes. Josh goes on to explain:

> The lines are there to protect you from hitting others. So God has given rules to protect and provide for you. He wants to protect your most important sex organ—your mind! Hebrews 13:4 says, "The marriage bed [should

be] kept pure." But heavy petting and beyond will go into your long-term memory.

Josh tells of a young man who said sex with his wife was hurt by memories of old affairs: "Josh, I've got ghosts from former relationships. I experience reruns in my mind."

He talks of how biblical rules protect young people from distrust and suspicion, from the fear of sexually transmitted diseases. And he speaks of the "mass media lies" about sex. "The average teen sees 9,230 acts of sex on TV a year, 93,000 by age twenty! What influences you is fiction. You will never see the price of sex. Have you ever seen anyone get a sexually transmitted disease on TV?" he asked a group of hundreds at a retreat last summer. Only a few hands went up. "It'll be a great day when J.R. (of "Dallas") gets VD!"

He uses more than Scripture, humor, and common sense to make a case. What's most moving are comments by young people speaking truth with power: "I just couldn't take the pressure anymore. My boyfriend kept pressuring me for sex. The longer I resisted, the more I kept thinking, *What am I waiting for anyway?* You know I didn't have an answer—it seemed everyone else was enjoying it so I finally gave in. Now I know why I shouldn't have had sex, but now it is too late."

Are the youth in your church equipped with answers? Isn't it the job of your church to give them? The Nazarenes think so. Thousands of their five thousand churches have shown the videos to their youth groups. With what impact? "It was by far the best thing we've ever done," said Rev. Kevin Dunlop of the First Church of the Nazarene in Anderson, Indiana. "Attendance grew each week. The first night we had thirty, and by the end, it went to seventy. One session dealt with pressure lines guys and girls will use." Like what? "All the other girls are doing it," says a boy. "Then you won't have any trouble finding someone else!" he hears. The youths laugh and cheer.

And churches in some cities are staging a Why Wait? youth rally with Josh McDowell in person.

If your church will write a letter on its stationery, a free sample of the videos will be sent. Or you may order them for $79 for the youth series and $159 for the eight-part parent series. Write Why Wait? P.O. Box 1000M, Dallas, Texas 75221.

39 A n s w e r

Clean Teens Say No to Sex

One thing I like about Pope John Paul II is that he boldly preaches a strong, clear biblical stand on sexual morality, unlike too many clerics.

But what chance is there that Americans—especially the young—will listen? The objective data looks grim, but I see reason for hope.

More than half the nation's youth have had sexual intercourse by the time they are seventeen. A million teens get pregnant annually, and half of these giving birth are under age eighteen. Births to unwed teens soared 300 percent since 1970 and teen abortions number 400,000 a year. So far, only a few religious leaders have taken a forceful position, such as Catholic Archbishop Roger Mahoney of Los Angeles. He recently asked the 3 million Catholics he shepherds "to boycott all businesses that sell or rent X-rated material. Find out which video stores in your community uphold family values. I encourage you to shop there."

By contrast, thrice-married Dr. Ruth appears on nightly TV backing adultery, premarital sex, sodomy, and legal prostitution. In this context, it is extraordinary and immensely encouraging to see signs that young people themselves are calling for sexual purity.

"Sexual freedom includes choosing to say no," says Marie Lee in an issue of *Young Miss* magazine. "I have many friends who admit they wish they had not started having sexual relations in their teens."

More significant is the emergence of an organization in Modesto, California, called Clean Teens, which was founded by Kirk McCall, then an eighteen-year-old college sophomore. Interestingly, Clean Teens began as an antiporn group, but as Kirk had spoken to twenty-five church youth groups and schools, he shifted his focus to sexual purity, saying, "There's not as much opposition to it as I expected."

"Though 80 percent of guys and two-thirds of girls have experienced sexual intercourse, people are agreeing with us. There is a real desire for abstinence among youth. When they hear positive reasons for abstinence, they say, 'Now I know why to say no.'"

An important book in preparing him for this ministry was Josh McDowell's *Why Wait?* It reviews the reasons teens are involved sexually—physical, emotional, environmental—and then gives reasons on the same grounds for chastity. As Kirk summarizes the rationale to youth: "Chastity is important because of the physical repercussions of promiscuity. AIDS, sexually transmitted diseases, and teen pregnancies are rising every year. Those who go along with sex before marriage for emotional reasons find emotional problems—guilt, frustrations, jealousy. And in the spiritual realm, it is obviously contradictory to be sexually promiscuous and to be walking with God." He quotes 1 Thessalonians 4:3, "It is God's will that you should be holy: that you should avoid sexual immorality, that each of you should learn to control his own body."

One of the people who challenged him at one of his appearances was LaJeana Goss, nineteen: "I'm a virgin who believes abstinence is good. But it is the girls who have to say no. It is time for guys to stop asking!" She was applauded and got an offer to join Clean Teens' board. Now she's more articulate: "My abstinence is the best thing LaJeana can do for LaJeana and for the future husband I love. My husband will have to match up to my Lord, who gave Mary Magdalene honor and dignity. He will have to love me enough to wait."

Zaharia Chawinga, sixteen, says the purpose of Clean Teens "is to reach kids who are hurting and give them peers to talk to. We are teens talking to teens, and we are being trained by a psychologist on how to counsel them. So many kids are so messed up. A friend of mine who was very promiscuous has gotten pregnant and has dropped out to have a child."

I wish Clean Teens had been started earlier.

For information, write Clean Teens, P.O. Box 918, Modesto, CA 95353.

A n s w e r **40**

Pro-Lifers Should Promote the Adoption Option

There is a scandal in the pro-life movement. Almost none of the babies being saved from abortions are being given up for adoption. It is as if the pro-life forces are only pro-life up until the birth of the baby—with little pro-life concern after birth.

There are an estimated one million families who want to adopt a baby. Yet the number of adoptions of babies unrelated to the parents has fallen from 89,200 in 1970 to about 50,000 a year now—at the very time that illegitimacy has soared from 399,000 in 1970 to 1,165,000 in 1990. Only about 30,000 of those babies are adopted. The rest are foster children or are older, handicapped children. The nation's largest adoption agency, with offices in thirty states, Bethany Christian Services, based in Grand Rapids, Michigan, placed only 805 children for adoption in 1992, 147 of whom came from abroad!

Consider the three hundred thousand babies born to unmarried teenagers. Personally, I am glad the children were born rather than aborted. But that should not be the end of the story. The issue should not just be whether the child lives, but what kind of a life it—and the mother— have? Surely it is better for a baby to grow up in a stable home than to be brought up by a single mother who is more girl than woman, whose prospects for education, work, and marriage are all sharply diminished by giving birth out of wedlock.

An unmarried mother keeping a baby is twice as likely to be poor as one whose baby is adopted and seven times as likely to be on welfare, says the National Center for Health Statistics. Nevertheless, of the 185,000 women counseled in Christian Action Council crisis pregnancy centers, only 4 percent relinquish their child for adoption. And Birthright centers, counseling 300,000, "are lucky if one percent" are adopted, says its national director, Denise Cocciolone:

> This does not make sense. They are getting pregnant at much younger ages, yet what they say is, "I don't want to give up nine months of my life to give my baby to someone else." Sometimes, you can discuss it and say, "This would be the most selfless act of your life." But we don't want to be part of any situation coercing her. As soon as you do anything they see as pressuring, they walk out. We are a single issue organization. We are trying to keep girls from killing their babies.

That single-issue focus is the problem. I asked Mrs. Cocciolone whether Birthright introduced pregnant women to families who had adopted a child or to adults who had been adopted as children to learn the other side of the issue. She said no. Giving information on the adoption option is not coercion. It is love.

A study by Professor Edmund Mech of the University of Illinois indicates that when pregnant women are counseled by social service agencies like Bethany who know about adoption and have a positive attitude toward it, 42 percent of pregnant mothers will decide to relinquish their baby, only 3 percent will abort, and 55 percent become parents. But if their orientation is to abortion, like most Planned Parenthood clinics, 60 percent choose abortion, 36 percent become parents, and 4 percent choose adoption. Groups oriented toward parenting will have 5 percent choose abortion, one percent select adoption, and 94 percent opt for parenting. Thus, *the type of counseling given is crucial.*

The Christian Action Council said it had learned this lesson and recently offered adoption training to some CAC directors. The trainer was Anne Pierson, who directs "Loving and Caring" and heads the Christian Maternity Home Association. Since 1972, about half of her mothers gave children up for adoption. Says Pierson:

> The swaying element is helping them understand that either decision involves pain. Placing a child for adoption is painful. A girl is

choosing to grieve. But parenting is painful, too. The decision is not to avoid hurting. Second, I say, "Take *I* out of your conversation. Place the child's life before your own." Most realize it is important to have a mother and a father and have a secure future, which most cannot offer. But it is an act of love to place her child. Those women should be honored, not scorned.

What is the result? She asked 160 mothers who made that choice and got 91 replies. Some 88 percent were so pleased with their decision that they would recommend adoption to another person. One said, "I learned what love really is." However, Christian Action Council adoption rates have *not* increased since Ms. Pierson's seminar.

If you would like more information, Ms. Pierson wrote an eight-dollar manual, "Helping Young Women Through the Adoption Process," and a two-dollar pamphlet for pregnant women, "Looking at Adoption." Write her at 1817 Olde Homestead Lane, Suite H, Lancaster, PA, 17601.

The question remains: Why aren't Christians—particularly those who see abortion as murder—trying to convince pregnant women, like the 337,000 unwed teenagers who give birth in 1989, to give their children up for adoption to intact families headed by a husband and wife?

There are three problems. First, the stigma of being an unwed mother has largely disappeared. The culture's conventional wisdom is that it is OK for women to bring up children alone. But reality is much harsher than this wisdom suggests. Unwed mothers who keep their baby are two and a half times more likely to end up on public assistance than those who give them up for adoption. Only 60 percent of those with babies get a high school diploma versus 77 percent of those who relinquish the child.

Perhaps most important to the woman, her odds of eventually getting married increase by 50 percent if she gives the baby to adoptive parents! This data comes from interviews with eight thousand women aged up to forty-four on what happened to them if their first child was born out of wedlock.

Very little real love is shown to unwed mothers. The pro-life and pro-choice people fight over the birth of the baby, but how many expectant mothers have the option of moving into a licensed, small group shelter with loving care? Close your eyes and guess how many centers there are in America for one million unwed mothers a year. Did you guess 175 residences that can serve two thousand women?

In fact, there were 201 homes serving 6,000 women in 1966; but by 1981 they shrank to 91 aiding 1,676 women. They are growing slowly again due to the National Committee for Adoption (NCA). Why? NCA knows that 40 to 50 percent of the residents will relinquish the babies—twenty times the average! "Adoption is a by-product of a caring approach for pregnant women in crisis," says William Pierce, director of NCA. "The percent of white women who place their children for adoption who receive counseling is 21 percent; but only 2.7 percent of those who did not get counseling do so."

Sadly, women need such centers to get away from parents who pressure them to keep the baby—as a punishment, or because they want to be grandparents. Boyfriends have the same negative impact. Babies of women who don't talk to parents are three times as likely to be adopted, and five times as likely among women who avoid the boyfriend!

In Seattle, the Washington Association of Concerned Adoptive Parents places five hundred children for adoption. "We have the solution. We even allow the birth mother to choose her family!" said its director, Janice Neilson. "The mother wins. The family wins. The baby wins." That's why Pierce says, "A residential center is needed to give the woman a milieu in which she can objectively make a decision." To learn more, write Bill Pierce, NCA, Suite 512, 2025 M St. NW, Washington, D.C., 20036.

41 A n s w e r

Straight Talk about Homosexuals

President Clinton is running into a concrete wall in trying to lift the military's ban against active homosexuals in the armed forces. Good. It is one political promise that should never have been made.

There is much misinformation about homosexuality. Begin with the assertion in *Newsweek* in 1992 that "like the population at large, the armed services are 10 percent gay." That figure is based on flawed Kinsey research. A quarter of the men he interviewed were prisoners who often practice homosexuality due to a lack of women. A 1991 study of the National Opinion Research Center found only "2 percent of sexually active adults reported being exclusively homosexual or bisexual during the year preceding the survey."

Another common assertion is that gays "are born that way." A study by Simon LeVay, a professed homosexual, seemed to show a genetic difference. By examining the brains of thirty-five male cadavers, he found that a cluster of nerves in the hypothalamus was twice as large in heterosexual males as in homosexual males. Robert Knight of the Family Research Council counters, "Since behavior can alter brain patterns, the size of the nodes may be the result, not the cause, of homosexual activity."

More important, there is substantial evidence that many homosexuals can change their sexual orientation. Masters and Johnson report a 79.1 percent immediate success rate for their patients who attempt to discontinue homosexual activity, and 71.6 percent success rate after five years.* (Like alcoholics, some do slip back into their old life-style.) There are 130 ex-gay groups helping men and

* William H. Masters and Virginia Johnson, *Homosexuality in Perspective.* (Boston: Little, Brown & Co., 1979), 402.

women change their sexual orientation, and five thousand have been successful. In fairness, however, most gays can not remember having anything but a same sex attraction. And thousands of gays have tried to change but can't.

The nurture versus nature debate cannot be proven either way. A more important question is whether homosexuality is desirable and healthy—something society wants to encourage as equally valid as heterosexuality. The answer is clearly no—and not just because two-thirds of those dying from AIDS are gay. A recent study published by the Family Research Council in Washington, D.C., of 5,246 obituaries in sixteen homosexual newspapers found that the average age of those dying from AIDS was thirty-nine. But the average age of those dying from all other causes is only *forty-one*.

Why? Gays are three times as likely to have alcohol or drug abuse problems. And homosexual youth are twenty-three times more likely to get syphilis and other sexually transmitted diseases than heterosexual youth. Why? They have vastly more sexual partners. A 1978 study found 43 percent of white male homosexuals estimated they had sex with five hundred or more different sexual partners, and 28 percent had more than a thousand.

An American Psychological Association study in 1984 reported that average homosexual promiscuity did drop after the onset of AIDS. Instead of seventy partners a year, they had fifty partners. And most of those partners are strangers. "Homosexuals are notoriously promiscuous," Commander Craig Quigley of the Navy told *The New York Times* in January of 1993. To heterosexual sailors, this is not only repugnant, but having to shower with gays is an invasion of privacy. It is as if female soldiers were forced to shower with young males.

"I cannot think of a better way to destroy fighting spirit and gut U.S. combat effectiveness," said David Hackworth, who has eight Purple Hearts and is the most decorated living American veteran. In the *Washington Post* (June 28, 1992: 65), he cites examples of inappropriate behavior, such as a gay commanding officer who gave combat awards to his lovers who had never been on the line.

> I saw countless officers and NCOs who couldn't stop themselves from hitting on soldiers. The absoluteness of their authority, the lack of privacy, enforced intimacy, and a twenty-four-hour duty made sexual urges difficult to control. The objects of their affection were impressionable lads who, searching for a caring role model, sometimes ended up in a gay relationship that they might not have sought. Sure banning gays from defending their country is discriminatory. But discriminations are necessary when a larger public purpose is being served.

In combat, men must be able to "trust one another totally," Hackworth concluded.

E. L. Pattullo, a retired director of Harvard's

Center for Behavioral Sciences, writes in *Commentary* that "substantial numbers of children have the capacity to grow in either direction." He calls them "waverers" (December 1992).

To the extent we want to strengthen "the institution of the family and to the extent parents have an interest in reducing the risk their children will become homosexual," Pattullo says there's reason to resist "the movement to abolish all societal distinctions between homosexual and heterosexual."

42 A n s w e r

"Transformation" Helps Gays Change

Anthony Falzarano, thirty-five, gave the most extraordinary Christian testimony I've ever heard in church—how he fell into homosexuality, was delivered of it, and has since created Transformation, a ministry to men and women in Washington, D.C., who want to escape what Paul called "shameful lusts."

He told Christ Our Shepherd—his own congregation—that his father "was a weak person, an absentee father." As a neglected eighth child, in a poor immigrant family, Falzarano felt, *I am not worthy.*

> At age twelve, I was molested by my brother; he later committed suicide. A man picked me up and offered me money for sex. I fell into a group of people who were paying for that [including Roy Cohn, the famous attorney from the McCarthy hearings who recently died of AIDS]. He took me in as his kept boy.

He was a millionaire with a Rolls Royce,
Palm Beach, Europe—whatever I wanted.
Sin began as a cobweb and then became
chains. I was in bondage. I stayed in a gay
life-style for nine years. I saw everything.
When you see someone say they are gay, they
are not gay, are not happy at all. For a time,
when you first come out, you have an identity, after growing up when you have no
identity whatsoever.

"I got involved in male prostitution," Falzarano
continued. "A client came to see me. We had a sexual fall together. He got out of bed and said, 'I
have sinned, and I have caused you to sin.' I said,
'What are you talking about?'" The man pointed
to various verses in Scripture. Falzarano, who had
a nominal Catholic upbringing, had never seen
the verses that say homosexuals cannot "inherit
the kingdom of God." Though he was making
thirty thousand dollars a year as a prostitute, he
"could no longer do this for money."

But he remained active for five more years:

I slept with four hundred men in nine years.
Slowly, I stopped the promiscuous sex which I
was addicted to. Then the oddest thing happened. I went home for Christmas. Diane was
my cover for my homosexuality before my
parents. She was a dear friend. Christmas evening in 1982, I was in church and the Holy
Spirit spoke to me: "You will marry Diane."

Living in the gay life-style, that was totally ridiculous to me.

But the thought kept returning to him, so he wrote Diane. "She called me, saying 'You will think this is weird. But that's what a voice told me!' We were engaged by February," and married in October.

A few months after their marriage, when Diane was pregnant, a former boyfriend called and said, "'You'd better get tested.' I said, 'For what?' 'Because I am dying of AIDS.' It hit me like a ton of bricks. I slept with four hundred people. I must be infected! But the test came back negative.

"From that point, I made a covenant that I would never sleep with another man. The Lord healed me like that. I told him I was sorry for the sin in my life. But the thoughts did not go away. Four years into our marriage, I was an addict to pornography." Someone suggested he go to a ministry for ex-gays in Baltimore called Regeneration. At his first meeting, 1 Corinthians 6:9-11 was read, which goes beyond saying that male prostitutes and homosexuals won't inherit the kingdom of God. "And that is what some of you were. But you were washed, you were sanctified" by Jesus. In other words, a total transformation is possible. Regeneration introduced him to books to help him understand the root causes of his homosexuality—a weak father, sexual molestation, etc.

Five years ago he became convinced "God spared me" from AIDS (which has killed thirty-five of his friends) for a purpose: "to reach out to the thirty thousand to thirty-five thousand homosexuals living within five miles of this church, to tell them, 'You don't have to be in bondage.' After nine years of being on the top in the gay life, I know how miserable and unhappy these people are." But he says, "For many years we could not get support from churches. You can go to a cocktail party, and say 'I am a recovering alcoholic or drug addict,' and people say, 'Praise the Lord!' But if you say, 'I am a recovering homosexual,' they, like, leave! This is what has to change."

I went to a Transformation meeting attended by twenty men and women. The most moving part of the evening came when they broke into three small groups for "confession." Chris, a male prostitute, poured out a ghastly tale of being tied down as a little boy by his mother and uncles for sex. Another youth visibly shuddered when asked, "Why are you here?" He could not talk about it.

Richard, thirty-one, left Toronto to come to Transformation. "I am a child emotionally," he said. He'd had sex with two dozen men, but "it has gone down a lot. I'm getting help here I need. My church wouldn't help me."

Why not? Don't churches believe the Scriptures that say people can change? To learn more about ex-gay ministries, call Exodus International at (415) 454-1017. It is a national umbrella for 130 organizations helping people out of homosexuality and lesbianism. They will refer any caller to the nearest local ministry, such as Transformation in Washington, D.C.

Build Future Leaders

Do you see glimpses of real leadership in a son or daughter? Perhaps you have witnessed initiative, selflessness, or courage. Some years ago my wife, returning from swim practice with our sons, told me of an incident involving John, then only seven years old. The door to the candy machine at the YMCA was broken and consequently ajar, and a boy of about twelve or thirteen was handing out candy bars to his friends. John walked up to the kid, looked up at him, and demanded, "What are you doing? Those candy bars aren't yours! You have no right to steal them. Cut it out!" John was no physical match for the older boy, but his boldness, his loud voice, and the possibility it might bring adults to the scene intimidated the young thief, who ran.

This year John graduated from Duke University with a Master of Arts in Public Policy. In many respects he is much the same as that little boy—unshakably honest and perfectly willing to confront his father or anyone else with a tough, reasoned point of view. No one else in our family has earned a master's degree, and we are proud of him. However, we are even more pleased that he has learned three keys to leadership: rock-solid integrity, a willingness to take risks, and communication skills.

What can we as parents or friends of young people do to encourage such sparks of leadership?

First, of course, we must praise whatever leadership, courage, or risk-taking we may observe in a young person. John was actually quite shy. When he said he was thinking of writing for his high school newspaper, he added that he doubted he could do the work. I said, "Look, I make my living as a writer, and I know you can write. And being a reporter is fun. You can interview anyone you want!"

Second, we must encourage the young person as he or she dares to take risks. John plunged ahead, nervously at first. As he achieved, his confidence grew. He wrote about many subjects for his school paper, then for the local daily paper while in high school. In college he earned money by covering high school sports for a local paper. During two summers as an undergraduate, he was an intern for a Washington political newsletter.

Third, we must let the budding leader lead in his or her own direction. Will John become a journalist like his dad? *No!* His writing experience convinced him he'd rather be *making* public policy than writing about what others are doing. Nevertheless, the writing was good training. "If one had to name a single, all-purpose instrument of leadership, it would be communication," writes John

Gardner in his book *On Leadership,* which I describe in Answer 43. Gardner adds, "Most of the communication necessary for leadership can be taught. Young potential leaders should gain exceptional command in both writing and speaking of their own language and, in an interdependent world—workable knowledge of a second language."*

Conventional wisdom has it that leaders are born, not made. *This is not true.* The skills needed to lead can be learned. Sadly, few young people today are learning those skills. In my three decades as a journalist, I've met no man more qualified to teach about leadership than John Gardner. As Secretary of Health, Education and Welfare during Lyndon Johnson's presidency, he helped create Medicare and the first federal aid to education and fashioned the policy that desegregated the South by threatening to withhold federal aid from cities that did not comply.

Gardner tried to convince Johnson to end the Vietnam War. When he failed, he resigned and took on a big risk in the wake of riots that were sweeping through dozens of cities in the 1960s— he created a National Urban Coalition to bring white and black leaders together in cooperation in cities where few knew each other. Later he created Common Cause, a citizen's lobby of 250,000 that worked to reform the financing of political

* John Gardner, *On Leadership* (New York: The Free Press, 1990), 166.

campaigns. And at the age seventy-seven, Gardner wrote *On Leadership* while teaching at Stanford University.

A fourth step, then, parents can take to inspire any budding young son or daughter is to give them a copy of *On Leadership*. It is packed with wisdom and insights on world leaders, written by an outstanding leader himself.

Some Colleges Nurture Values

A fifth step parents can take to help their children become leaders is to help them consider the moral dimension of leadership. How? Have your high schoolers take a look at colleges that consciously attempt to nuture *values* and *character* as well as academic skills and extracurricular prowess. Answer 44 tells about the Templeton Foundation Honor Roll for Character-Building Colleges. It is a list of about a hundred colleges and universities that "go beyond academics and instill the development of character and moral values."

Frankly, not many of these institutions are left. Virtually all private universities were founded by religious idealists, but most are decades or centuries past those animating forces. Harvard and Princeton, for example, were founded to train clergy! Duke University, my alma mater, was founded more recently, in the 1920s, as a Methodist institution. I loved my years there. I have sent two sons to Duke, and I interview Duke applicants as a volunteer. Duke has appeared on the Templeton

Foundation Honor Roll. However, in 1992 I wrote
to my alumni director:

> Duke seems to have forgotten half of its
> motto, *Erudito et Religio*. Where is there any
> sign of religion or morality on campus, other
> than the chapel (which towers 210 feet above
> the campus)? My oldest son, Adam, was an
> undergraduate at Duke, and the roommates
> he had his first two years regularly brought
> women into his room for sex. What was
> Adam supposed to do? Sleep in the library?
> *In loco parentis* has disappeared, and you have
> replaced it with nothing. I think you need
> to go back to single-sex dorms and curfews—
> at least for those parents who want such an
> environment for their children. Also, I was
> appalled at the percentage of drunks I saw on
> campus one Saturday night. I went to my fra-
> ternity (Theta Chi) and was stunned at the
> scene of debauchery—beer flowing an inch
> thick on the floor, a high percentage of inebri-
> ated students, and lots of smashed windows
> and beer bottles everywhere. Do you honestly
> think you are providing any moral guidance
> to the undergraduates at Duke? You are train-
> ing young people to be promiscuous drunks—
> while giving a superb academic education.
> One index of the problem I am trying to
> describe might be seen in the number of abor-
> tions given to undergraduates. How many stu-
> dents get abortions in a year, and how does

that compare with, say, 1975, 1980, and
1985? What does the Methodist connection
mean at Duke? Nothing but history, as far as
I can see.

Laney Funderburk, the alumni director, wrote
back:

I suspect you will get little argument from anyone at Duke about student excesses. . . . Duke
students today are under far fewer constraints
than we were. You and I remember women's
dorms closing hours, no opposite sex visita-
tion, a no-alcohol policy and chaperons
required for parties. *In loco parentis* was alive
and well in our day. It is not on college and
university campuses today. . . . You strike a
very responsive chord with me, and, I dare
say, many alumni and friends of Duke would
like to see a higher moral tone here. I could,
of course, say the same about society generally. I am impressed by annual exit surveys of
seniors . . . over a period of seven years. In
responding to a question asking if they ever
cheated, 85 percent have consistently
responded "never." Furthermore, more than
two thousand undergraduates annually do
some sort of community service. . . .

Note that he did not challenge my charac-
terization of the sex and drinking. Nor did he
answer my question about how many abortions

there are, or offer any reaction to the idea of rein-
stating the old rules for parents requesting them.
Instead, I got only the rationalization that *in loco
parentis* is no longer alive "on college and university campuses today."

Wrong. Geneva College in Beaver, Pennsylvania,
still has the traditional rules, as do many other
colleges that honor their religious roots: Wheaton
College in Wheaton, Illinois; Asbury College in
Lexington, Kentucky; Calvin College in Grand
Rapids, Michigan; Taylor University in Upland,
Indiana; and the University of Notre Dame in
South Bend, Indiana, to name a only a few. As
noted in Answer 45, Boston University has demonstrated it is possible to reinstate a residential hall
guest policy that sharply cuts overnight visitors of
the opposite sex by giving roommates the freedom
to say no. Alumni of other colleges should demand
similar changes.

Look for a College with an Honor Code

An important criterion to apply in helping a son or
daughter choose a college that will nurture moral
leadership is to ask these questions:

- Do you have a functioning honor code?
- Does it cover lying and stealing as well as
  cheating? (Few do.)
- Do students administer its sanctions, or is
  discipline handled quietly by an administration so that alumni influence can save the
  guilty? (Few are totally student run.)
- What are the punishments?

Washington & Lee University and the University of Virginia (two institutions ranked high on *U.S. News and World Report*'s 1993 list of best colleges) have two of the strongest honor codes in the nation. Answer 45 gives details. If a student is caught stealing a wallet, cheating on an exam, or lying to a professor at Washington & Lee, that student is *expelled*. There is no "suspension" for a semester. That's a tough sanction. It is made perfectly clear to new freshmen. And the result is life changing. "It made me realize that integrity is worth something," said an executive vice president of Mutual Insurance of New York, who learned the importance of ruthless honesty at Washington & Lee. He believes this was a key to his rise in the corporate world.

43 A n s w e r

Strong Leaders Must Be Developed

At the time this nation was formed, our population stood at around 3 million. And we produced out of that 3 million perhaps six leaders of world class—Washington, Adams, Jefferson, Franklin, Madison, and Hamilton," writes John Gardner in his book *On Leadership*.* "Today our population stands at 245 million, so we might expect at least eighty times as many world-class leaders—480 Jeffersons, Madisons, Adamses, Washingtons, Hamiltons, Franklins. Where are the Jeffersons and Lincolns of today?" The answer, Gardner is con-

---

* John Gardner, *On Leadership* (New York: The Free Press, 1990), 166.

vinced, "is that they are among us . . . unawakened leaders, feeling no overpowering call to lead and hardly aware of the potential within."

Gardner is a modern Jefferson: a former spy for the U.S. in World War II; author of seven books; a former foundation president; secretary of Health, Education and Welfare in the 1960s; founder of three major organizations, including The Urban Coalition, Common Cause, and Independent Sector; and now a professor at Stanford University.

He wrote the book for "young people who dream of leadership." He concludes that specialization and the professions "draw most of our young potential leaders into prestigious and lucrative non-leadership roles."

With a remarkable sweep of illustrations—from Gandhi and Churchill to Florence Nightingale and George Bush—Gardner outlines the qualities needed for leadership which go far beyond vision and communication skills. In contrast with managers, leaders "think longer term—beyond the day's crises, beyond the quarterly report," and they "reach and influence constituents beyond their jurisdictions." Indeed, the leader may have no organization at all. Nightingale "exercised extraordinary leadership in health care for decades with no organization under her command." Churchill "tried out for leadership many times before history was ready for him." Leaders "think in terms of renewal," and articulate the shared values of a people, realizing that "values decay over time." Bush is cited for his skills in "unifying" after his election by meeting with opponents—Michael Dukakis, Senator Robert Dole, his chief rival for the nomination, and with Jesse Jackson. Those reconciling skills were most visible when Bush fashioned an extraordinary consensus of world leaders against Saddam Hussein's takeover of Kuwait.

However, Gardner dismisses "charisma" as being too vague a quality to be analyzed. Instead, he puts a spotlight on "trust, a quality whose importance is widely ignored by academics," and "willingness [eagerness] to accept responsibility." Both qualities can be developed in the very young.

When Golda Meir, later prime minister of Israel, was age eleven living in Milwaukee, "she organized the American Young Sisters Society, a group of schoolgirls who raised funds for children who could not pay the nominal sum charged for textbooks in the Milwaukee public schools," he writes.

Gardner's book is already having a powerful influence. It has become a textbook for the training of young leaders. For example, Chi Psi Fraternity held a day-long conference at which quotes of his book were used to spark dialogue to help train student leaders of thirty-eight colleges.

"We cannot expect top leaders, working alone, to make the system work without the help of many others throughout the society," said one quote. "Most of the leadership that can be called effective involves a number of individuals acting in a team relationship," said another quote. They helped fraternity presidents understand the "empowering the followers form of leadership," said David Hopkins of Chi Psi's staff. He said, "The classical form of leadership has followers beneath him on an organization chart. In servant leadership, the leader supports his followers and is beneath them, empowering followers to do the work."

During the meeting, fraternity officers from different colleges broke into small groups to role-play that type of leading. Two were assigned to be brothers who got drunk and smashed windows, and the president was asked to build a consensus on handling them, said my son, John, who was there. When a drunk denied responsibility, others said they saw him do it. The president asked, "Do you think it is fair that we should pay for the windows?" a question that gently pushed them to accept responsibility.

Roger Pilc took a leadership course with Gardner, who now teaches at Stanford University. "What impressed me most was Gardner as a human being. His attitude was a humble one—not one who had been a big cheese. He was very accessible, and asked for suggestions on how to run the class."

One disappointing aspect of the book is that Gardner gives few illustrations of his own leadership. He doesn't tell, for example, how he got schools in the South to desegregate by withholding federal aid from them. But that is material for a future John Gardner autobiography!

44 *A n s w e r*

Colleges Need to Teach Character and Morality

In speaking to three hundred students at Geneva College, I said, "I'm going to ask you a question, but I want you to close your eyes, so that no one is embarrassed to answer it honestly. How many believe that it makes sense for a person to live with someone before getting married?" Only a half dozen hands went up.

Though Geneva is officially deeply "committed to the development of a Christian perspective," I was pleasantly surprised to see its character-building impact in today's hedonistic culture, where on most other campuses, males routinely spend the night in dorms with females—unheard of in my student days, 1958–1963. Roommates must choose between ejection or forced voyeurism.

Promiscuity on college campuses has led naturally to a sevenfold hike of unmarried cohabiting couples (from 430,000 couples in 1960 to 3 million now). Its consequences are disastrous. "Yale University sociologist Neil Bennett . . . found that cohabiting women were 80 percent more likely to separate or divorce than were women who had not lived with their spouses before marriage," said *Psychology Today* in July–August 1988.

That is secular evidence St. Paul was right in writing, "It is God's will that . . . you should avoid sexual immorality; that each of you should learn to control his own body in a way that is holy and honorable, not in passionate lust like the heathen,

who do not know God" (1 Thessalonians 4:3-4).
Yet most colleges—even hundreds founded with
clear Christian goals—have abandoned the
attempt to strengthen student character.

Fortunately, there are signs of a move back to
higher moral standards. John Templeton, a Rhodes
Scholar from Yale and a Presbyterian who became
a wealthy man, has created a "Templeton Foundation Honor Roll for Character-Building Colleges"
to "honor those schools which go beyond academics and instill the development of character and
moral values."

The process to choose those honored is the same
as used by *U.S. News and World Report* to choose
"America's Best Colleges." Presidents of every college or university were asked to nominate five to
twelve schools that "best exemplify good character
building with a strong emphasis on moral values."
That was defined as institutions "where students
may learn the fruit of the Spirit" named by Paul in
Galatians 5:22-23 (love, joy, peace, patience, kindness, goodness, faithfulness, gentleness and self-
control)—"as opposed to the seven deadly sins
named by St. Gregory" (lust, anger, drunkenness,
greed, gluttony, pride, and jealousy).

Dr. Verne Kennedy, a former president of Bel-
haven College who conducted the survey for
Templeton, said Honor Roll colleges should "be relatively free of drugs. Encourage the Golden Rule:
'Do unto others as you would have done unto
you' not 'Do unto others what profits you most.'
Encourage students to participate in religious

activities and develop a strong faith in God" versus colleges that "ridicule religion."

In the first year, leaders of some 693 of 1,447 institutions made nominations. Three colleges stood out as "the best of the best": Wheaton College in Illinois, and Taylor University and Notre Dame in Indiana. Others ranged from Brigham Young, a Mormon school, to West Point, Virginia Military Institute, Baylor University, and many small Protestant evangelical colleges like Geneva, Asbury, Calvin, and Houghton. Only a few institutions made the *U.S. News* and Templeton lists: Wake Forest, Davidson, Berea in Kentucky, and George Fox in Oregon. For a current list and brief summary of Templeton colleges, write Marketing Research Institute, 715 South Pear Orchard, Suite 25, Ridgeland, MS 39157.

A second sign of hope is that Boston University has adopted rules not seen since the 1960s that sharply limit students from having guests of the opposite sex overnight.

At Boston, visitors must sign in from 8:00 A.M. to midnight and are expected to leave the residences by 1:00 A.M. Monday through Friday and by 2:30 A.M. on Saturday and Sunday. Students may request an overnight guest privilege after receiving the consent of their roommates. But this may happen only five times per semester. The roommate helps control the situation.

The fact is, "no one has come near five visits per semester. The average is 2.1 visits," says Dean Herbert Ross. Before the policy was instituted in 1989, there were three thousand overnight guests of the eighty-five hundred students in the residence halls any given weekend. Now there are no more than a thousand who do so.

And there are many side benefits. "Vandalism took a dramatic decline. And student satisfaction with the quality of the environment, which was under 50 percent, is now 65 to 70 percent," said Ross. And though the number of student applications dropped slightly the year after the new policy got a lot of publicity, it is now higher than ever. Parents and students are voting with their applications *for a more moral campus.*

Of course, such rules spark protests from students who claim they became adults at age eighteen. But as a parent who paid the tuition bills for three of these "adults," I agree with the father who wrote Boston dean Norman Johnson, "There are many silent students who are thankful you are doing what you are doing, and many parents as well."

Two suggestions: First, alumni who see the need for change should write their college president. Second, Templeton's measure of "character building" could stand to be improved. Why not poll alumni to see which institutions have the highest percentages of people who serve others and whose marriages last?

A n s w e r **45**

Honor Is a Vital Ingredient in a W & L Student

When my wife and I visited our son John, a freshman at Washington & Lee University in

Lexington, Virginia, I came away determined to write about its honor system, initiated by General Robert E. Lee, president from 1865–1870 of what was then known as Washington College.

The importance of the system was clear to John who explained, "I lost my wallet. But a week later it was returned, with fifteen dollars I forgot was there." What if all America's students could learn about integrity like that?

The thought returned with power as I read with growing dismay about the ethics of Supreme Court nominee Judge Douglas Ginsburg. While owning $140,000 of securities in a cable TV firm, he wrote a brief as an assistant attorney general favorable to the industry. He claimed to have participated in dozens of cases that went to trial, but they were done by subordinates. He'd spent only an hour of his life arguing a case in court.

Then came the bombshell that he had used marijuana as a Harvard professor of law as recently as 1979. Sleazy ethics clouded one hundred top Reagan appointees, an unprecedented number. Three special prosecutors were examining former White House aides and even former attorney general Meese. But when the president named Judge Anthony Kennedy to the Supreme Court, he said that, like retiring Lewis Powell, Jr., Kennedy "is known as a gentleman." Integrity has begun to be seen as more important than ideology.

Since Justice Powell earned his B.S. and law degree from W & L, I wondered if the honor system was a factor in his character formation, and asked him. He explained: "My values were formed in a Christian home before I got there. But they could have been corrupted. If I had gone to another school, where, because of the competition, people cheat, I might have been tempted to join the crowd. But there was no temptation to cheat at W & L."

Why? There's only one penalty for a person who cheats: expulsion. W & L's "White Book," given to every freshman, says the system "is one of mutual trust—trust among students, faculty, administrators, and townspeople that persons attending Washington & Lee will not lie, cheat, or steal. We do not think it is too much to ask that students do their work, represent themselves truthfully, and claim only that which is theirs."

Brad Root, then president of the student body who also ran the Executive Committee that reviewed infractions, briefed freshmen and asked them to sign a pledge of honor. "If you do not believe in honor, you have the option to excuse yourself from the university," he said chillingly.

The presentation must have been powerful, for there were no reported violations that fall. But the previous year there were twenty-three investigations, eleven closed "fact-finding" hearings, and five guilty verdicts. Four were appealed and were given open trials with student jurors picked at random.

Executive Committee members took on the role of prosecutors. The accused asked law students to aid in their defense. Two were found guilty—of shoplifting and using a false ID to buy liquor. And two were acquitted of charges of plagiarism and property destruction.

Two aspects of W & L's system are rare, even among the several dozen colleges with enforced honor codes. First, it is totally student run. (An appeal is possible to administrators at West Point or Annapolis.) Second is the "single sanction" of expulsion found also at the University of Virginia. At W & L the only appeal is through a public "trial," in which a jury of students makes the final decision—not the administrators.

What's the rationale for that, since offenses vary in seriousness? "A student has made a contract with his fellow students that he will not lie, cheat, or steal. To do so is to forfeit the right to be at the university," declared James Socas, past chairman of UVA's Honor Committee. "Once a person shows a willingness to compromise his honor, he will do it again," said W & L's Executive Committeeman Pat Scheafer. "This generates more respect for the system." Also the task of judgment is easier. "We are obligated only to prove guilt or innocence. It is not our obligation to decipher the penalty. All know the penalty," says Root.

But the benefits are also extraordinary. "Even the stores in town don't ask for an ID when you cash a check," says our son John. "Professors don't supervise classes taking exams. Bikes or computers can be left anywhere."

Justice Powell recalls, "W & L had a good football team in the early fifties. Scholarships were given. But there was a cheating scandal and eleven football players were expelled. So athletic scholarships were abolished."

Dean John Elrod says, "The only thing alumni worry about is how the honor system is doing." Does it have an impact on them after graduation? "It made me realize that integrity is worth something," says Gray Castle, executive vice president of Mutual Insurance in New York. "Even if we can rely on a technicality to get out of paying a claim, we won't do it."

What if all colleges had an honor code? "Integrity would become a norm of the society," Castle said. The University of Maryland is studying the W & L model. Others should too. For more information about the plan, write Executive Committee, W & L, Lexington, VA 24450.

Encourage Selfless Service

The economics of Jesus seem upside down: "If you give, you will get!" as *The Living Bible* puts it very bluntly. And the next sentence is even more striking: "Your gift will return to you in full and over-flowing measure, pressed down, shaken together to make room for more, and running over. Whatever measure you use to give—large or small—will be used to measure what is given back to you" (Luke 6:38, TLB).

This is a basic eternal principle. In my experience, it is a rule that works almost like the law of gravity. If I reach out to serve, it is *I* who will be blessed by the experience. But how many of our youth know this truth? Very few. Why? It is a truth that can be known only as it is experienced. It is a truth few parents, few churches, and even fewer schools create the opportunity for young people to learn.

Do you doubt that assertion? What did any of your children do this week to help others? Did they sacrifice any time for anyone else? If not, why not? If by serving others they will reap a reward, "full and overflowing," why are there so few servants?

Selflessness is not a natural emotion. Selfishness is natural. (A best-seller a few years ago was *Looking Out for Number One*. No one that I know of has written a book called *Love Your Neighbor as Yourself*.) Selflessness must be demonstrated by the adults in a child's life before he or she can begin to grasp the concept. A mother will see herself as selfless in much that she does for a child. But the child takes that behavior for granted. The parent must be generous with someone *outside* the immediate family, and the child must be a part of the experience, for the child to begin to feel the joy of giving that Jesus speaks about.

This final chapter suggests practical opportunities parents might use to awaken in their children a sense of mission to serve others—and also to awaken in them a recognition that "much is required from those to whom much is given" (Luke 12:48, TLB).

The Angel Tree Project

A toddler, age three and a half, gave one of her toys to the child of a prisoner in 1992. Why? "I don't want a child to go without Christmas," she explained. That is the essence of the Angel Tree Project, now a decade old, described in Answer 46.

In more than ten thousand churches across America, volunteers—many of them parents who involve their children—pick a paper angel with a child's name on it off a Christmas tree in the church. Written next to the child's name and age is a gift that the child hopes to receive for Christmas. Some 140,000 prisoners signed up 265,000 of their children in 1992, giving names, addresses, and phone numbers to their prison chaplain. The chaplain then turns the names over to Prison Fellowship, a ministry of forty-nine thousand volunteers working to bring the love of Christ to "the least of these" in prison.

Prison Fellowship volunteers distribute the children's names to churches in or near the communities where the inmates' families live. Church volunteers then purchase gifts, which are given to the children as if from the parent who is a prisoner.

"It was exceedingly amazing to me that your help went not in your name, but in my name," said an impressed inmate in Georgia.

"I have signed up for this program three years running and have never been disappointed in the love and joy your volunteers bring my sons," exclaimed another prisoner.

"I think this is the best thing that's ever happened for prisoners and their children," said a third.

Prison Fellowship tells of a fifteen-year-old named Emily in Overland Park, Kansas, who spent a year saving three hundred dollars to purchase gifts—roller skates, educational toys, Legos, and stocking stuffers—for four-year-old twin boys and their older sister. She found the children needed coats and enlisted three other church families to donate warm clothing. Clearly, Angel Tree is a wonderful way for parents to teach children the spiritual principle, "Give, and it will be given to you."

Maryland's Student Service Alliance

Kathleen Kennedy Townsend, the oldest daughter of Robert Kennedy, has created a curriculum and trained hundreds of teachers in Maryland to get high school kids involved in serving others. Under her prodding, in 1985 Maryland became the first state to require local school systems to offer credit to students who perform community service.

"Maryland students are tutoring younger students in English, math, and science," she exclaims proudly.

In the preface to the *Maryland Student Service Alliance* draft instruction framework, it states,

> They have weatherstripped and rehabilitated houses, and tended animals in the zoo. They have planted sea grasses to save the Chesapeake Bay, and tested pollutants in our streams. They have acted as peer counselors, created plays about drug and alcohol abuse, and entertained senior citizens with songs and fashion shows. They have been huggers at Special Olympics, and they have served meals at shelters for the homeless.
>
> These are not simply nice things to do. They develop the character necessary for a vibrant national life. . . . At our best we teach the young to care for others, their parents and their children. We hope others, in turn, will do good unto them and care for their parents and children. Thus we create a strong nation, and develop the habits of personal and social responsibility.

Unfortunately, several years ago only three high schools in the state were getting virtually every student involved in community service. One of these was Francis Scott Key High School, described in Answer 47. On a statewide basis, "less than 2 percent of all kids were taking advantage" of the law giving course credit for volunteer work, Mrs. Townsend told me.

Therefore, in 1992 she persuaded the Maryland State Board of Education to *require* every student to do some community service. It is not a big requirement—seventy-five hours to be completed in one's junior-high and senior-high years. Yet this community service requirement is very controversial. Forty state legislators have signed a bill to cancel it, and hearings were held on it in 1993. The legislators argue that volunteerism has to be voluntary, or it is meaningless. These opponents apparently do not recognize the value in training young people to form habits of volunteerism.

My youngest son, Tim, took a high school humanities course in Bethesda, Maryland, that required him to do community service. He volunteered to bring Meals on Wheels to elderly invalids for several weeks. "It was the best thing I ever did in high school," he said later. "I had no idea what the circumstances are that some people have to live with." The requirement nudged him to venture into an unknown world of community service. He gave his time, but he received much more—a new compassion for the elderly poor.

How are children to understand the value of

serving others, if they are not introduced to it?
That has to be the task of schools as well as that of
churches and parents. I take my hat off to Kathleen Kennedy Townsend for having the vision to
create the Student Service Alliance—and to convince Maryland to require some community service of all high school graduates.

Could your high school use the curriculum
Maryland has developed? Write the Maryland
Department of Education at the address given in
Answer 47.

Youth With a Mission

Of course, it is the primary obligation of parents—
not the schools—to encourage our children to
serve others in need. Our oldest son, Adam, took
on a variety of volunteer activities while in high
school. But in college, he developed a hunger to
introduce others to the gospel. We told him about
Youth With a Mission (YWAM), an evangelistic
effort in which even high school kids can work
abroad on short-term missions. And we offered to
help him pay the modest sum required to cover his
room, board, and supervision.

Answer 48 tells what his experience was like,
attending a YWAM Discipleship Training School
for three months and then giving two months of
service in Kenya. Adam grew tremendously
through his mission experience.

Only about half of the seventy-four hundred full-
time staff serving with YWAM are Americans or
Europeans. The rest come from the Third World.

They work with fifteen to twenty thousand "short termers," people who give at least two weeks of service, which can be in this country as well as abroad. Of that number, four to five thousand take the middle-ground approach of Adam—the three-month Discipleship Training School followed by two months of service. You might ask YWAM to make a presentation to your church youth group. Their phone number is in Answer 48.

Urbana '93

If your son or daughter is uncertain about whether to serve as a missionary on either a short-term or long-term basis, the best single step he or she can take is to attend an Urbana Missions Conference. Sponsored by InterVarsity Christian Fellowship only once every three years at the University of Illinois campus, the next one will take place from December 27 to 31, 1993. At Urbana '90 some 19,500 attended; more than a thousand had to be turned away. By the time this book is published, there will be little time left to sign up. Call (608) 274-7995 to find out if space is still available, or begin now to plan for 1996!

Answer 49 describes the Urbana experience. Some fifteen hundred missionaries go to the campus in Champaign, Illinois, to meet students, and 250 of the larger missionary agencies set up exhibits that describe their work. In 1990, 12,457 students made some level of commitment. Almost all pledged to "unreservedly give myself to Jesus Christ as Lord of the universe" and committed

themselves to "studying Scripture, giving financially to and praying for God's work, and developing a life-style that reflects kingdom values." Fully
4,018 pledged to go on a summer mission project;
1,975 committed to a service of one to three years;
2,256 signed up for career service; and 4,475 more
said, "I will become involved in global missions
and commit myself to clarify how and when."

Pledges are easy, of course. But how many actually go? John Criswell, InterVarsity's director
of public information, says, "It often takes ten to
twelve years to make a decision. They have to finish
school, pay off debts, make decisions on marital
relationships, and become clear about the will of
God for their life. But a survey of Urbana '84 decision-
makers in 1988 found that 43 percent had begun or
planned to begin some form of missionary service."
After a decade probably more than half have begun
the most selfless form of service: laying down their
lives to respond to Jesus Christ's Great Commission
to "make disciples of all nations."

The Peace Corps
What if the young person in your family is idealis-
tic but does not feel called to be a missionary?
Indeed, are *you* bored with your work? Would you
like to take a couple of years off to be a teacher in
the former Soviet Union or Eastern Europe or
India? Why not consider the Peace Corps? Answer
50 tells about the joy 130,000 returned volunteers
feel for the opportunity the United States gave
them to offer selfless service in the Peace Corps.

When John Kennedy created the Peace Corps, the average age of those going was twenty-two. In 1993, it is thirty-one. And those going to the former Soviet Union are forty-one years old on average. Why? Countries are requesting volunteers with specific skills. For example, Russia is looking for people who have had experience in small business development or who have a Master of Business Administration degree. Virtually none of the first three hundred to go could speak Russian. But the Peace Corps provides an intensive three-month immersion in whatever language one will need in the country where one will serve.

What are the odds of going? In 1992, there were 17,438 applications for 3,300 positions. But the more experience you have, the greater are the chances you can serve. In 1992 there were seven thousand volunteers serving in 104 countries.

America's idealism lies dormant. But it has been awakened anew by President Bill Clinton's call to create "National Service," a domestic version of the Peace Corps modeled somewhat after the Civilian Conservation Corps, which gave 2.5 million young people in the Depression "the opportunity to support themselves while working in disaster relief and maintaining forests, beaches, rivers, and parks, " said Clinton. "The lesson of our whole history is that honoring service and rewarding responsibility is the best investment America can make." As an alternative to repaying student loans, young people could work as National Service volunteers, as Clinton envisions it.

The President says, "We'll ask young people to work to help control pollution and recycle waste, to paint darkened buildings and clean up neighborhoods, to work with senior citizens and combat homelessness and help children in trouble get out of it and build a better life."

At this writing it is unclear whether Congress will create National Service. In any case, most volunteering by young people awaits a call to action by parents, church leaders, teachers, and locally elected officials. However, home bears the primary responsibility for awakening in our children a call to serve God and others. As Martin Luther King said in 1965, "Family life not only educates in general, but its quality ultimately determines the individual's capacity to love."

What will you do to help your family catch the vision of service to others?

46 *A n s w e r*

Angel Tree Gives to Prisoners' Children

Out of the anguish of one man in prison at Christmas has emerged a project that is enabling thousands of Americans to share the purest form of Christmas joy with the neediest of people—children of prisoners. The man is Chuck Colson, the first to go to prison in the Watergate scandal. Chuck recalls,

> I remember vividly what Christmas in prison was like. It was painfully frustrating, my heart aching for my family. And my anguish was compounded by the realization that my wife

and children were suffering more. I am convinced that the ones who are hurt the most
are the little children. If Daddy is in prison
and Mommy is on welfare or working two
jobs to make ends meet, Christmas is just
another day of the year. How tragic that this
should happen to one child, let alone thousands. Christmas marks the birth of Christ—
God come to earth in the person of Jesus.
When we remember these little ones, we are
in the most eloquent way, remembering him.*

Yet in Christmas 1992, 265,000 children of
140,000 inmates experienced a miracle—getting
gifts chosen by their mom or dad in prison, but
bought and personally given by loving hands of
church volunteers from 10,672 churches sponsor-
ing Angel Tree Projects across America, a program
sponsored by Prison Fellowship.

When Mrs. Cathy Lund of Polk City, Iowa, delivered gifts to homes in the inner city of Des Moines,
she told the children, "Your father must love you
very, very much, because he sent your name to us
so we could go out and get these gifts for you, since
he couldn't be here." The presents she delivered
included some new clothes, a toy for each child, and
large food baskets for each family. It was often very
moving. One boy did not want to wait till Christmas
to tear off the wrapping. He squealed with delight

*Taken from promotional material put out by Prison
Fellowship.

when he saw an electric train and said, "Did you know my dad loves trains?"

In Washington, D.C., one of the biggest Angel Tree Projects in 1988 had a Christmas party sponsored by forty churches for twelve hundred children of eight hundred prisoners at Lorton, a massive prison outside of Washington. The kids, guardians, and volunteers came in shifts in a masterwork of organization. But at one point, the presents of an eight-year-old boy could not be found. He was the most tranquil person as volunteers scurried about. He said confidently, "If we don't find them today, I know we will find them before Christmas. They're from my daddy." (They were found.) Stuffed in amidst the gifts were comic books that told the real story of Christmas, the birth of Jesus.

Even the hearts of TV news personnel melted. They interviewed the wives of prisoners who thanked Prison Fellowship, and some said they were frankly surprised and pleased that so many suburban church volunteers came to the inner city "to lift up the name of Jesus."

In the Milwaukee area, Debbie Reygo said that taking Angel Tree presents to children "was pretty difficult for me. It was my first experience in going to the inner city. But I was very well received. One of the families sent a child out to guard my car," a late model Lincoln.

Her church, the large Elmbrook Church in Waukesha, gave about fifteen hundred dollars worth of gifts to forty-nine children. Prison Fellowship guidelines limit amounts to be spent. Sadly, there were more donors than children. Many inmates with children are skeptical and don't sign up for the Angel Tree Project.

But what does it mean to those who do participate? Thanks to Chaplin Walter Morris of Wisconsin's Foxlake Correctional Institution, I was able to get firsthand reactions of convicts by phone interviews.

"My kids were thrilled. They got their first two choices and two alternate gifts," said James Myers, forty-nine. "In previous years I have been there to go shopping and provide these things. They were given in my name as if I had been able to do it. It makes me feel that people care."

Mike Eggleston, thirty-six, said, "Project Angel Tree is for inmates. It is made up entirely of Christians. The people got my wife's name, address, and phone and asked what they could give. They could not have been there two minutes. There was no glory in it for themselves. My boy, who is nine and a half, was surprised. He's old enough to appreciate the effort of so many. He said, 'Thank you! It means a lot!'"

Paul Sage, twenty-seven, said, "It is a big thing to us. These people who spent their money to buy gifts for our children have every reason *not* to like us. Many are not in good financial situations themselves. Yet they were willing to share with us. It was encouraging to my wife, who has not always felt that positive about people in the community. It is a way of showing true Christian charity. This is people giving without expecting anything back. It's real giving. It is special." What's more, some volunteers will continue seeing the kids all year long.

Why not plan not to get your church involved next Christmas? Write Mark Morgan, Prison Fellowship, Box 17500, Washington, D.C. 20041.

47 *A n s w e r*

Community Service Encourages Teens to Help Others

Maryland's Student Service Alliance has gotten teens involved in serving others.

"Before it began, I hated to come to school," said Amy Robertson, seventeen. "But now I want to go to school to do community service. I feel like I helped somebody else who would have been ignored if we had not done something to help. When I get out of school I still want to help people."

That transformation of attitude is remarkable since Amy and her classmates in community service are not college-bound, but general education students at Francis Scott Key High School in rural Union Bridge, Maryland.

It all began in a class that combined math with social science where students designed a logo for placemats as Christmas presents for the elderly in a nursing home. They then used their skills in measuring, planning, and budgeting to mass produce 225 laminated mats with fancy foil paper. The old people were invited to a school lunch where they were given the mats and were stunned by the students' gesture. "Some put it on their bedside table, or hung them on the wall," said Amy. "We thought they'd use them in the dining hall, and were amazed that they were hung up. It was nice that something so small was so important. Somebody cared about them."

The experience was so satisfying, the students went back to decorate the nursing home for Easter. And students developed other service ideas. Chris Simms, fifteen, decided to organize a fund-raiser for Armenian earthquake victims. He set up a card table and volunteers to ask for contributions at three different lunch waves for a week. He raised $259. "Before I got into community service in school, I was bored," Chris said. "I never saw a reason to come to school. Now I got a reason to come here. I was helping people."

Amy heard that and added, "When I came to Francis Scott Key in my junior year, I was a smart aleck, a little brat. I tried to fit in as the class clown. But it's better if you do positive things. I have a lot more friends now. You get close to people you work with." Even at her after-school job at Sizzler steak house she convinced the restaurant to feed two hundred homeless people on Thanksgiving, and she helped serve.

Though Francis Scott Key is in the middle of cornfields, far from the homeless in Baltimore or Washington, the kids got the faculty to donate peanut butter and jelly so kids could make sandwiches for the homeless. What inspired that was the experience some students had of working at the Baltimore City Franciscan Center, which feeds the homeless. It was also inspired by the afternoon activity of a community service conference sponsored by the Maryland Student Service Alliance of the State Department of Education. In the morning, awards were given out to the most creative student initiatives and kids heard what other schools were doing.

Francis Scott Key then came up with the idea of inviting special education students to spend a day in a "regular" school. A boy named Tony explained, "Our students were 'buddies for a day.' At lunch they were given hats. After lunch we showed them around to the nursery school, the greenhouse; what they really liked was driver's ed."

Jennie Tregoning, a member of student government, explained how student government transformed a traditional spring fling into community service projects, "Some went to an old folks home to clean windows and garden. Others collected cans and donated the money raised to the Kidney Foundation. And some kids did things with homeless children." The freshman class got inspired to make calendars for nursing home residents, with key historical dates and quotes from the presidents.

The woman behind this burst of activity at forty-five high schools in the state is Kathleen Kennedy Townsend, eldest daughter of Bobby Kennedy. With grants from the Abell Foundation, she has fashioned a series of teacher training institutes and drafted a superb curriculum that provides a rationale and suggestions on how to awaken student interest in community service that range from preventing crime, serving the disabled, and promoting literacy to ending drug abuse and cleaning the environment. "The ethics of service has been a hallmark of our democratic heritage since America's inception," says the curriculum's foreword. "Thomas Jefferson wrote in 1793 that 'a term of duty in whatever line he can be most useful to his country is due from every individual.'"

To help students in your area become what Jefferson called a "participator in public affairs," send twenty dollars for the curriculum to Maryland State Department of Education, 200 West Baltimore Street, Baltimore, MD 21201.

A n s w e r **48**

YWAM Changes Lives

"Youth With a Mission changed my life," said my son Adam, who was nineteen when he returned from five months as a YWAM missionary in Kenya and Tanzania. My wife and I saw many changes immediately. Adam was trimmer, more disciplined, more loving, and more committed to serving the Lord. But only when I interviewed him for this column did I learn the changes he spoke of were quite different; they were in the areas of personal Bible study and witnessing.

"I've grown up in a church that always stressed the importance of a Christian feeding on the Word of God, and had done some Bible study on my own. But YWAM encouraged a consistent time set apart to learn and grow spiritually, which cannot occur unless you study the Bible daily. If you aren't reading God's love letter to you, you do not know what his will is for your life. You can't have a relationship with anyone unless you spend time in communication," he said. "I've never been a shy person. But before YWAM, I would only share my faith with someone with whom I had a deep personal relationship—a teacher or friend. I was not making an effort, as the Bible teaches, to share the message of the gospel with others on a daily basis. The Great Commission is not a suggestion but a commandment to go into all the nations and make disciples. The Greek word for *nations* means people groups—not physical geographic locations. So Jesus wants me, as a college student, to share my faith with other students."

Youth With a Mission is big—7,400 full-time volunteers and 15,000 to 20,000 "short-termers," serving in 200 permanent bases in 116 countries. That's three times the 7,000 Peace Corps volunteers now serving in 104 countries. What's it like? "YWAM brings both hands of the gospel around the world," Adam said. "There's a mercy ministry— clothing and food distribution, aid to disaster victims—help in physical, practical ways. Secondly, it brings the gospel through evangelism, open-air meetings, and drama."

Every YWAM volunteer must raise his/her own costs to serve. In Adam's case, the cost of a two-month Discipleship Training School (DTS) and five months of room and board in 1985 was nine

hundred dollars (plus travel costs). Today the cost
is two thousand to three thousand dollars. "At the
core of the school is healing broken relationships
between students and God—essential for anyone
to share their faith," he said.

A typical day during DTS begins at 5:30 with a
quiet time for Bible study, memorization, and
prayer. There are two teachings in the morning
and one at night. Afternoons involved work, such
as fixing or painting walls. Once a week there was
a "mini-outreach." One day they helped build a
medical clinic by digging ditches for pipes and
pouring concrete. Another day they gave away
powdered milk and Bibles in downtown Mombassa.

Yosef, a seventeen-year-old Muslim boy, watched
them aid an old woman and asked why they cared
for a stranger. Andrew, a Kenyan, explained how
God transformed his life from being a thief to a
person giving away milk in a park. Adam
explained the Scriptures and led the boy to Christ.

After DTS ended, Adam and ten others made
YWAM's first outreach to Tanzania. Staying in a
small Pentecostal church, they'd spend the day witnessing in mud hut villages or in government
housing projects. At night Adam preached in
many churches of different denominations. He was
"surprised by the many nominal Christians that I
met. They're in church weekly, but had made no
commitment to Jesus. It was just like America."
Teams of two YWAMers would spend an hour or
two with a non-Christian family answering many
questions.

One evening, after an exhausting day, Adam and Omari, a former Muslim, felt led to go back to a government apartment that had sewage flowing in ditches outside. They were drawn to a young, muscular construction worker who asked them in. Adam found a new way to tell how God loved man. Standing at his full six feet, two inches, with Omari translating, he said, "Pretend that I am a giant, and that I love all of those do-do [insects] on the ground there very much. I have a plan for their life, but all they can see are my big toes. The do-dos do not see me as I am. So I become a do-do myself. With miracles, I show I am God and care for them, but that I require a certain amount of obedience. I show that temptation can be overcome. And one day I allow myself to be stepped on. Then I physically rise from the dead, proving I was a giant who had become one of them. . . . Jesus is not a man only. He is God. Jesus has made a difference in my life and he can in yours. But it is like someone giving you a ring as a gift. You must decide to take it."

The young man said, "Two days ago I cried out to God, 'There is an emptiness in my life. I have been drunk or on marijuana every night for the last two weeks. Mohammed can't be who he claims to be. There must be more to Jesus.' I asked God to send a messenger to me within two days, and you have come within two hours of that." He then accepted Jesus.

God may be calling you, even if you aren't young. For information, send three dollars to

YWAM International, Box 4407, Kailua Kona, HI 96745. Or call 1-800-424-8580, ext. 2293.

A   n   s   w   e   r *49*

Urbana Introduces Youth to Missions

"Jordanians had heard of Christianity and were not hostile to it—only misinformed," said Shane Bennett, twenty-two, who went to Jordan as a short-term missionary recently. "They believed Christians had three gods—God, Jesus, and Mary. They equated Christianity with America. And on TV they see Americans engaged in all kinds of immoral or unethical things that would never be allowed in Islam. In meeting Americans, they assume we are all that kind of people."

The next spring, Shane went to Bangkok for a similar exploratory effort to help missionaries figure out how to best penetrate that culture in order to plant new churches. Another goal of his "Caleb Project" is to persuade U.S. students to serve the Lord abroad.

How did Shane decide to be a modern Caleb sent to spy promised lands? In 1984, he was one of eighteen thousand students who attended Urbana '84, a five-day student missions convention held at the University of Illinois's Urbana campus every three years by InterVarsity Christian Fellowship, an interdenominational ministry active on eight hundred mostly secular college campuses.

"I really went to hear the speakers, like Billy Graham. I went open but pretty ignorant. It was the first time I had considered God caring about the whole world. I never thought of the billions of people who had never heard the gospel, or the complexities of getting it to them across the barriers of politics, race, and language," Shane told me. "At first I wondered how God could allow such a grave situation to exist—of people dying without a chance to know him. Then I thought, *How can the church allow this?* In America we spend money on great buildings that mostly sit around not doing anything. And I was a part of that."

Some nineteen thousand students attended Urbana '87. Billy Graham, Tony Campolo, and other noted people spoke. More important, 160 mission agencies responsible for three-fourths of the forty thousand full-time Protestant missionaries were there to recruit. Wycliffe Bible Translators, which has translated the Bible into 264 tongues and is working on 800 more, sent fifty-five missionaries to Urbana to have the students "consider us as one of their options," said Karen Lewis of Wycliffe. "Urbana is our largest single recruitment effort."

With forty-seven hundred U.S. missionaries, Wycliffe is bigger than all twenty-six mainline Protestant agencies put together, and is geared to showing how much help they can give to those called by Jesus to go to "the ends of the earth. We offer seminars on public speaking, on how to write letters to communicate the concept of a partnership, and will send letters as a third party to their list of possible supporters." However, every missionary must raise his or her own financial support.

Mission recruiting is done on a one-to-one basis. In fact, students whose preliminary applications show the strongest interest are sent an eight-page questionnaire in advance. Those are sent out to mission agencies so that personal appointments can be made before Urbana.

InterVarsity has learned a lot about how to conduct Urbanas, having staged sixteen of them since 1947. In 1984, 4,683 attendees signed a statement saying, "I believe that it is God's will for me to serve him abroad and I will pray and make inquiry to that end." Another 10,153 said they felt they had a "part in God's plan for the world" and would "actively seek his will for me by increasing my awareness and involvement in world missions." Of those fifteen thousand, an estimated five thousand have done short-term mission work and one thousand have made career decisions to serve. Those who don't go are asked to help send others with monthly checks for at least three years.

But follow-up is the key. The 3,308 who pledged to give received the names of three Urbana alumni interested in going, and were urged to pick one with the message, "You have made a commitment. Be accountable."

The Reverend John Kyle, who has directed three Urbanas, is optimistic. "There is a trend away from 'me-ism' to 'we-ism.' This generation is concerned for others—especially for the 3 billion people who have not heard the name of Jesus," he said. "We will focus on the need for urban missionaries. Cities are where most people live. Yet they have been largely ignored by missionaries. And the solo missionary is out. Teams of people will go and work together."

After one Urbana conference, some eighty students from forty-five different campuses launched a National Student Mission Coalition with the extraordinary goal of reaching the 2.5 billion "frontier people" who have never heard the Christian gospel with understanding.

But what difference do missionaries really make, anyway? And what can eighty kids do?

In Africa, even after twenty years of independence for most countries, "85 percent of all schools are there because of missions," according to Dr. Ralph Winter, director of the U.S. Center for World Missions in Pasadena, California, which serves forty-two different mission agencies. "And six hundred hospitals in India plus 50 percent of all nurses in India are missionaries."

Missionaries in Japan have had an influence far beyond their numbers. Christians are in the forefront of all social causes, such as outlawing prostitution in Japan. Many of the key schools in Japan were formed by missionaries.

The Jewish theologian Samuel Sandmel is quoted by the *Encyclopaedia Britannica* on the impact of the first Christian missionary, St. Paul: "One needs only a glimpse at the history of Europe and America since the veritable rediscovery of Paul by Martin Luther to discern the permanent and imperishable. It was out of a renewed emphasis upon Paul that there developed, albeit in secularized form, those attitudes toward the individual, toward freedom of the conscience . . . which made the transition from the middle ages to modern times."

Thus, when missionaries dream of taking the gospel to a thousand different Buddhist peoples speaking different tongues, to the Chinese who have two thousand dialects, to the three thousand Hindu groups of peoples and four thousand Muslim groupings plus the five thousand tribal clusters, they are dreaming of unlocking an enormous human potential as each of 2.5 billion people awaken to the realization that they are important in God's eyes.

Few churchgoers realize that only 10 percent of all the 150,000 to 200,000 Protestant and Catholic missionaries in the world are reaching out to non-Western peoples. Most can be found in such areas as South America, not India or China. That's why the National Student Mission Coalition (NSMC) is putting its primary focus on "meeting the need of unreached peoples," as Rob Larkin put it. Elected as one of the three officers of NSMC, he and his wife have studied Chinese.

When he spoke at Wheaton College, he said, "I'm leaving in two years to work with the Chinese. I'd like you to pray about getting on that plane with me and actually serving the Lord overseas. Or stay here and pray for me and others directed to go and support us financially."

In his mind's eye is what happened a century ago, in 1886, when what became known as the

Student Volunteer Movement sprung up on American campuses. Some 100,000 students committed themselves to overseas missions. Only 20,500 actually went overseas, while the 80,000 stayed home and supported them.

That grass roots student movement had a multiple impact. The number of Protestant missionaries abroad jumped sevenfold overnight. Those who remained at home developed an interest in international affairs that led many into diplomacy. "The United Nations flowed from the power of that movement," says Dr. Winter.

But there has been no comparable movement into the mission field in a century. After World War II, a number of veterans who had been abroad decided to embark on missionary careers. But they are from another generation and are themselves ready to retire.

Indeed, there are thirteen thousand mission vacancies already and a need for another hundred thousand to enter new territory.

Can the new student coalition amount to anything? "Not since 1886 has there been this kind of a coalition," Dr. Winter asserted. "It's student led, and not InterVarsity or aligned with some denomination. It is friendly with all existing organizations, but beholden to no one. Its focus is exclusively on the frontier peoples. And it is alive."

Why not help send someone to Urbana '93 as a Christmas present? The cost is only $360 for room, meals, and materials. For more information, call (608) 274-7995, or write Urbana '93, Box 7895-M,

Madison, WI 53707-7895. The results could be marvelous.

A   n   s   w   e   r **50**

Peace Corps Is a Means to Serving Others

At midnight on the eve of the twenty-fifth anniversary of John Kennedy's assassination, I attended a moving vigil in his memory by former Peace Corps volunteers in the Rotunda of the U.S. Capitol. The big crowds had gone home. But the volunteers were still giving their time, speaking one by one, all night long. As fifteen of us listened, I wondered whether their sort of idealism could be found in today's youth.

In his inaugural address, Kennedy's words were stirring: "Ask not what your country can do for you, but what you can do for your country." The Peace Corps gave America's youth a practical way to respond.

"Kennedy's idea of patriotism was service of a different sort, not in foxholes, but in villages," wrote an ex-Peace Corps woman in an *Atlanta Constitution* article, read in the Rotunda. "This new patriotism called for a radical response of citizens to serve—not to shoot at—those in the Third World. A strong military was not the only line of defense." She spoke of how Kennedy's idea was "non-bureaucratic, small-scale, relying on volunteers at subsistence salaries in sharp contrast with military aid projects." They were goodwill ambassadors with a vision that "not muscle power, but idea power could change the world."

Hap Carr, a volunteer to Venezuela in 1969–1970 and to Brazil in 1971, talked of how he earned a master's degree in international relations and "thought I knew what the development process was all about." But when he said good-bye to his mother, "I was excited and scared. I had no idea what the Peace Corps was like or whether I could hack it."

In fact, Carr had no job description and felt so overwhelmed initially in a "Wild West kind of place" sixty miles from Caracas that he was grateful when he was asked by Venezuelans to play in a baseball game.

However, in time, he designed a garbage collection system, a city budget, a tax collection system—remarkable achievements for anyone, let alone a young volunteer. Not surprisingly, he married a woman he met there and has worked in international development ever since. "I learned to create my job and matched my skills for my environment. My experience with the Peace Corps set a standard for me through the rest of my life by which I judge the level of my commitment, my steadfastness." He concluded, "John Kennedy created the Peace Corps from nothing so that we could learn how much we truly have to offer."

President Bill Clinton could elicit a similar response from this generation's youth. He has called for a National Service Trust Fund to enable any student to go to college, and either pay it back at a small percentage of their income over time, or through community service as teachers, law enforcement officers, health care workers, or peer counselors, helping kids stay off drugs and in school. A Gallup poll in 1990 revealed that 58 percent of the nation's adults donate at least four hours a week to charity—up from only 30 percent in 1981.

But Clinton needs to be more specific. Why not call for an expanded Peace Corps both abroad and in the nation's ghettos and barrios at home? In fact, this is an idea Congress has pursued. In recent years, it has increased the number of Peace Corps volunteers to 7,000, toward a goal of 10,000. And a domestic counterpart, VISTA volunteers, has grown to 2,200.

Costs are not large. Peace Corpsmen live on a subsistence local wage of about $200 a month, and have another $200 banked for them—a cost of only $5,000 a year per volunteer. VISTA costs are $7,500 each. Yet there are many more applicants than are accepted. Clearly, both could be expanded at relatively little cost. The total Peace Corps 1988 budget of about $140 million is one-tenth the cost of a B-2 bomber. The administrative, training, and supervisory costs would not double as another 5,000 Peace Corps volunteers are added for $25 million.

These numbers could be multiplied many times over if President Clinton were to ask the presidents of every college in America to encourage students to serve the local needy.

Wooster College in Ohio is a model for an unpaid domestic Peace Corps. Some four hundred students choose to live together in twenty-eight different houses on the basis of their shared interest in a volunteer service activity. Examples: A dozen women spend hours each week at Every Woman's House Shelter caring for battered women and their children. A racially mixed group live in what they call The Dream House to promote interracial understanding. One house works with a juvenile detention center. "They are decent kids who need to be pointed in the right direction," said Erik Knorr, a Wooster student. "Our purpose is to get kids to interact with positive role models, to see that there are other options in life." Another group works with Habitat for Humanity to build a home for the poor to be sold at no profit and no interest. (Students at thirty colleges have Habitat chapters.)

America's potential for service is huge. What's needed is inspiration. It's up to parents, teachers, politicians, and other role models to show today's young people that they can make a difference.

A poll by the Barna Research Group in 1993 found that 57 percent of teenagers were asked to volunteer—and 90 percent responded affirmatively. The failure of young people to live out their faith by helping those in need may be due to the failure of older people to ask!

Some Final Thoughts

As any parent knows, our kids are growing up in a far more dangerous world than we did. The temptations of drinking, sex, drugs, and pornography, for example, are much greater and more enticing now. Some of today's temptations did not even exist in the 1950s or 1960s.

It is not impossible, however, to be a good parent even in times like these. We parents are still the most influential people in the lives of our children, and we are able to create the climate in which our children will thrive. If we are serious about taking our kids back from the world, what we need more than anything else is *a recovery of self-confidence on the part of parents.*

For example, a survey revealed that only 15 percent of mothers and 8 percent of fathers had ever talked with their children about premarital sex.* Why so few? Surely every parent knows this is a tough issue for their teenagers, and most

* E. S. Roberts, D. Kline, and J. Cagon: *Family Life and Sexual Learning of Children,* Vol. 1 (Cambridge, Mass.: Population Education, Inc., 1981).

parents would like to see their teenagers abstain from premarital sex.

Such a lack of self-confidence is totally unjustified. Based on interviews with seven thousand seventh- to tenth-graders, Dr. Stan Weed, president of the Institute for Research and Evaluation in Salt Lake City, concluded in 1992 that parents can make a big difference in whether their teenagers remain chaste. Parents who make a case for abstinence can be even more influential than a teen's peers! But if a parent lacks self-confidence and remains silent, the teen will be pushed toward the values of our modern permissive culture.

Without knowing about this research, my wife, Harriet, and I took an activist stance with our three sons. Instinctively we felt that our teenagers needed time to grow up, time for extra protection and nurturing, time to prepare for adult life. In chapter one I recommended David Elkind's 1984 book, *All Grown Up & No Place to Go*. If you haven't bought or borrowed it yet, do so as soon as possible. In the meantime, I'll repeat a statement of his I quoted earlier: "Every adult must do what he or she can to stretch out those adolescent years, offering both protection and wholesome nurturing."

That is the philosophy undergirding this book. After all, I have called it *50 Practical Ways to Take Our Kids Back from the World*. I have not proposed putting the kids in a monastery. Rather, I've suggested steps to delay worldly pressures—steps such as not allowing a son or daughter to drive until age seventeen, or keeping merchants from selling tobacco or alcohol to underage children, or using positive peer pressure to reinforce the idea that premarital virginity is the right decision.

For too long parents have deferred to the "experts," who often turned out to be quite incompetent. For example, parents agreed with experts on the need for sex education in public schools, but usually failed to examine the content of the curriculum. Those who have studied what is now being taught are frequently horrified. Although most parents do not want their kids to be sexually active, few have made the personal effort even to talk about chastity with their kids. Why? Perhaps they naively felt that the "experts" in school would be more persuasive than old Mom and Dad. *If we parents can recover confidence in our own moral standards, we will come a long way toward getting our kids back from the world.*

There *are* practical steps to take our kids back from the world. But we have to be willing to stand up to adolescent ignorance, petulance, and opposition. None of our three sons wanted the TV off all week long, but all of them developed musically, athletically, and academically as a result. And none of our sons wanted to wait until age seventeen to get a driver's license. But none of them had an accident at age sixteen or started drinking at that age or got a girl pregnant.

On the other hand, it is not enough to "just say no." Harriet, especially, invested extra energy to

provide alternatives for our sons that would promote healthy growth. She drove them to swim
team practice or music lessons or Little League.
That meant she did not work full time in their for-
mative years. And we drove junker cars and
"tented" on our vacations. We took our boys to
Sunday school and paid to send them to church
retreats. All of our kids learned to ski on those
retreats, but Harriet and I have never been skiing.
We couldn't afford it! We had spent our money so
they could go where they would have fun, but also
where they would hear a clear message on why
they should commit their lives to Christ.

Every parent has to make choices. We chose
steps for our kids that rejected worldly values, that
stretched out their adolescent years. Did we succeed in taking our boys back from the world? We
hope so, but it is too early to be certain—they are
only in their twenties. There are hopeful signs.
Throughout high school and college they were
involved in activities to serve others in need. Two
have been short-term foreign missionaries, and the
other has been a "Big Brother" to a young fatherless boy.

Being a parent is not easy, but we have found it
very rewarding. The fifty practical suggestions in
this book come from our experience as parents and
from my reporting as a newspaper columnist. They
are collected here with the hope that they may
offer other parents a running start on how to nurture children in these tumultuous times.

I offer them with a sense of humility. My final

thoughts about children are expressed in these
words of Kahlil Gibran:

> *Your children are not your children.*
> *They are sons and daughters of Life's longing for*
> *itself.*
> *They come through you but not from you,*
> *And though they are with you yet they belong not*
> *to you.*
>
> *You may give them your love but not your*
> *thoughts,*
> *For they have their own thoughts.*
> *You may house their bodies but not their souls,*
> *For their souls dwell in the house of tomorrow,*
> *which you cannot visit, not even in your*
> *dreams. . . .*
>
> *You are the bows from which your children as*
> *living arrows are sent forth.*
> *The archer sees the mark upon the path of the*
> *infinite, and He bends you with His might*
> *that His arrows may go swift and far.*
> *Let your bending in the archer's hand be for*
> *gladness;*
> *For even as He loves the arrow that flies, so He*
> *loves also the bow that is stable.**

* From *The Prophet* by Kahlil Gibran, copyright 1923 by
Kahlil Gibran and renewed 1951 by Adminstrators C.T.A.
of Kahlil Gibran Estate and Mary G. Gibran. Reprinted by
permission of Alfred A. Knopf, Inc.

Meet the Author . . .

It was a sermon I heard in 1981 that inspired me to begin writing my column "Ethics & Religion." The Rev. Everett (Terry) Fullam, to whom this book is dedicated, was preaching on the parable of the talents in Matthew 25. He asked the congregation a question: "What are *you* doing with your talents to serve the Lord? Don't tell me you are an usher. That is not significant Christian service." (I gulped. I was an usher, and that was all I was doing to serve Him.) "We will always have ushers," Terry said. "What I want to know is, what are *you* doing to take the talents and gifts God has given you that *make you unique as a person* to serve the Lord?"

I did a mental inventory. What *was* I doing that was unique? Well, I was writing a syndicated political and economic column on how to revive the old industrial states of the Northeast and Midwest. And I was selling (syndicating) it myself. How could that serve the Lord? Then I suddenly thought of all the boring church pages in America's newspapers. None would move anyone even to go to church, let alone live their faith in ways to serve others. "I bet I could write a column that would put content on that page," I mused. "And since I'm already a syndicated columnist, I'd have access to editors that other writers do not have. I could probably sell a number of my existing newspaper subscribers on a second column."

Then I began having second thoughts. "What am I thinking about? If I start writing about religion, many of my editors will no longer trust my judgment on political and economic issues. They will drop me!" (A prophecy that proved correct!) I had not gone to a seminary or even covered religion as a reporter. Pretty arrogant to talk about starting a nationally syndicated column about religion with no training or experience! Besides, I was already working sixty hours a week. "I don't have time," I told myself, as I dismissed the idea.

As if he were reading my mind, Terry continued his sermon: "Now, if you are having second thoughts about doing what the Lord has led you to consider doing to serve Him, remember that Moses had second thoughts about leading his people, Israel, out of Egypt. Turn to Exodus, chapter 4, verse 10. Moses is arguing with the Lord: 'O Lord, I have never been eloquent, either heretofore or since thou hast spoken to thy servant; but I am slow of speech and of tongue.'

"And look at the Lord's response," said Terry. "'Who has made man's mouth? Is it not I, the Lord? Now go, and I will be with your mouth. . . .'"

I gulped, and thought, "Well, I guess He would be with my typewriter!"

Michael J. McManus

Today "Ethics and Religion" appears in over a hundred newspapers nationwide. *50 Practical Ways to Take Our Kids Back from the World* is Mr. McManus's second book. His first book, *Marriage Savers,* was published in the spring of 1993, by Zondervan Publishing House.

Index

A